"Moon lovers and witches, rejoice! Author Elen Hawke has given us a wise, intelligent guide to deepen our awareness of ancient lunar mysteries. Her evocative meditations, gracious rituals, and practical magic skillfully incorporate the Goddess, Celtic Tree Calendar, Indian Lunar Zodiac, and so much more. *Praise to the Moon* is a book you will cherish and live by."

—Karri Ann Allrich
author of *A Witch's Book of Dreams* and *Cooking by Moonlight*

"At last . . . a book that truly gives the moon her due! Filled with rituals and brimming with recipes of magical possibility, *Praise to the Moon* provides everything necessary to harness this powerful energy for positive life change. It's a must-read for every serious practitioner on the planet!"

—Dorothy Morrison
author of *Everyday Magic* and *The Craft*

". . . A magickal addition to your library!"

—Suzanne Reinhardt Kuhn
owner of Morgana's Chamber, N.Y.C.

"This is the book for moon-lovers. If you are enchanted by that silvery orb, *Praise to the Moon* will guide you in the journey to understand her phases, to weave magick under her light, and to commune with her ancient and wisdom-filled nature. Ms. Hawke's careful research and lilting style has paid off in this lovely volume of moon-lore and mysticism."

—Yasmine Galenorn
author of *Embracing the Moon* and *Crafting the Body Divine*

ABOUT THE AUTHOR

Elen Hawke is a British witch who lives in Oxford, England, with her husband and a house full of animals. She has a grown daughter and son. Elen is a photographer, illustrator, and has been a professional astrologer for twenty-nine years and a tarot reader for twelve. These days, she divides her time between healing, teaching witchcraft, meditation, and chakra work, and celebrating the moons and festivals with the rest of the coven to which she belongs.

TO WRITE TO THE AUTHOR

If you wish to contact the author or would like more information about this book, please write to the author in care of Llewellyn Worldwide and we will forward your request. Both the author and publisher appreciate hearing from you and learning of your enjoyment of this book and how it has helped you. Llewellyn Worldwide cannot guarantee that every letter written to the author can be answered, but all will be forwarded. Please write to:

Elen Hawke
℅ Llewellyn Worldwide
P.O. Box 64383, Dept. 0-7387-0278-1
St. Paul, MN 55164-0383, U.S.A.

Please enclose a self-addressed stamped envelope for reply, or $1.00 to cover costs. If outside U.S.A., enclose international postal reply coupon.

Many of Llewellyn's authors have websites with additional information and resources. For more information, please visit our website at http://www.llewellyn.com.

Magic & Myth of the Lunar Cycle

PRAISE
TO THE
MOON

Elen Hawke

2002
Llewellyn Publications
St. Paul, Minnesota 55164-0383, U.S.A.

First Edition
First Printing, 2002

Book design and editing by Karin Simoneau
Cover art © 2002 by Chad Wallace
Cover design by Lisa Novak
Interior illustrations © 2002 by Matthew Archambault

Library of Congress Cataloging-in-Publication Data
(Pending)

Llewellyn Worldwide does not participate in, endorse, or have any authority or responsibility concerning private business transactions between our authors and the public.

All mail addressed to the author is forwarded but the publisher cannot, unless specifically instructed by the author, give out an address or phone number.

Any Internet references contained in this work are current at publication time, but the publisher cannot guarantee that a specific location will continue to be maintained. Please refer to the publisher's website for links to authors' websites and other sources.

Llewellyn Publications
A Division of Llewellyn Worldwide, Ltd.
P.O. Box 64383, Dept. 0-7387-0278-1
St. Paul, MN 55164-0383, U.S.A.
www.llewellyn.com

 Printed in the United States of America

For Rosie

CONTENTS

acknowledgments

Loving gratitude is due to the following people: my ever-supportive family and friends; Karin, my hard-working, meticulous, and patient editor; Karri Ann Allrich, whose friendship, humour, and encouragement are so valuable coming as they do from a fellow author who understands the ups and downs of the creative process; and, last but not least, The Children of Artemis (www.witchcraft.org) who have done so much to promote my work.

introduction

As I write this on June 21, 2001, it is the day of the Summer Solstice and a solar eclipse. Eclipses are powerful points on the moon's cycle, and during solar eclipses the moon temporarily blocks the energy of the sun, allowing us to turn inward and experience our lunar/earth selves, with all the mystery and magic that that implies. Today's eclipse is very important because, though the sun's entry into Cancer at Midsummer marks the beginning of his descent from power and the commencement of his journey into the dark half of the year, when the sun enters the moon's sign, Goddess and God are joined in the Sacred Marriage—a deeply spiritual and special event for pagans. Because the lunar sign of Cancer relates to nurturing, family, and the feminine mysteries, today's eclipse will prompt the unfolding of these qualities within us all and give us a chance to balance the male and female energies within ourselves—an appropriate time indeed to begin a book about the moon.

Along with celebrating the eight seasonal festivals, working with the moon's cycle is at the heart of witchcraft. We watch the moon grow from a thin crescent to a large glowing circle, then fade away into darkness once more. We time events so that they commence with the waxing moon, just as our ancestors did; we work our magic for increase as the moon grows toward full, and we decrease or banish with the moon's waning. Some of us may sow seeds, either symbolic ones representing new projects or real ones in the soil of our gardens, with the new to waxing moon, and most of us will want to reap our harvest or push for fulfilment of some kind at full moon, when the lunar force is strongest. There is a pattern to all this, a marking of celestial events that is ancient, though often disregarded by the inhabitants of our busy modern world with its restless outward activity, but the pattern is natural to ourselves and the other species on the planet, and can bring harmony and balance to our existence if acknowledged and followed.

This book is about observing those ancient cycles, and understanding their place in our lives and their relevance to witches practicing in a world that has forgotten many of the old ways of being. It is a world where for many of us the night sky is lit by a yellow sodium glare against which the heavenly bodies are dim; we time our lives by clocks and watches and urgent schedules—even the shops are often open twenty-four hours a day now. It is as though we have created a condition of perpetual daylight, constant busyness, which serves our solar selves at the expense of peace and reflection and the inward listening that we need if we would heed our instinctive promptings. We are in servitude to the Father and have forgotten the Mother. Even our patterns of menstruation and fertility have suffered. We need to discover and connect with the moon and her patterns once more if we are to find serenity and inner peace.

Within this book I will focus on each moon's phase in turn, exploring its inherent qualities and the relevant deities, and giving examples of pertinent rituals and magic. I hope this work will help witches and other pagans to better understand the lunar qualities that are at the heart of their practice.

It's also worth mentioning here the different yet similar role the Goddess plays in the lunar as opposed to the solar cycle. In terms of the twelve-month ritual year, she mates with the God at spring, and the divine child is conceived. During the summer months she nurtures both the crops in the fields and the child within her womb, then loses the God with the harvest in autumn. Then at Yule the God is reborn, and the Goddess moves toward Imbolc and the restoration of her Maiden state, ready for the cycle to begin once more. The lunar pattern is similar except that the transition from Maiden to Mother happens on a monthly basis, and the barren phase is much more apparent, relating to the Crone and old age rather than a nonfertile postnatal condition that happens to coincide with winter's harshness. As witches we observe both cycles: the smaller cycle marks our more immediate celebrations and needs, while the larger sequence encompasses the long-term projects we are working on during each year and toward which the monthly ups and downs contribute, while giving us a chance to focus on our spiritual and psychological growth. The two series are interrelated, yet can be viewed as separate and important in their own right.

But the way we experience the moon goes beyond the three faces of the Goddess. Each moon's phase will fall within a particular zodiac sign, which will influence the way we experience its qualities, and eclipses will modify the new or full moons on which they fall. Added to that, there are other lunar conditions that will leave their mark on us or alter our experiences, and among these are the twelve Celtic moons and the Indian lunar zodiac. All these will be explored within this book.

And, finally, a word about the God. In our society, which tends to view the moon as female, any spiritually based text about the moon is likely to be biased toward the Goddess. However, the God is ever present and is usually invoked along with the Goddess in lunar as well as seasonal rites. If I have seemed to concentrate more on the Goddess, this is only because I am writing about the moon, which is usually the focus for feminine deity to present-day pagans.

in the beginning

So long ago that it is beyond our imagining, when our earth was very young, she gained her only satellite, the moon. There are various theories as to how this came about. The first is that earth and moon were formed at the same time, born simultaneously from the fiery depths of the sun. Another theory surmises that the moon was an existing mass that came within the earth's orbit and was captured so that it became attached. The latest and most widely accepted theory is that some 4.5 billion years ago, another planetary body hit the surface of the earth, causing debris to fly out into orbit, coalescing into the moon.

Earth's satellite is the second brightest object in the sky after the sun, though one lights up the day and the other the night. As we tend to see sun and moon as a pair both naturally and mythically, it is therefore interesting, and symbolic, in a mystical sense, that both appear to be the same size, though the sun is actually many times larger and farther away. The moon itself is 239,000 miles from the earth. This may sound an enormous distance, but is in fact extremely close in terms of heavenly bodies, and allows us to clearly see the craters and other distinctive marks that give the moon its familiar face and features. Its closeness also means that its pull has a marked effect on all life on earth, affecting the tides and triggering hormonal and growth cycles within ourselves, the rest of the animal kingdom, and plants as well. Its roughly twenty-eight day cycle is linked to human menstruation and animal breeding. Its waxing and waning strongly affect our moods and energy patterns as well, and most people are at least subliminally aware of the buildup of tension or excitement as the moon nears full, and the corresponding draining away of vitality as she wanes again.

Although we can't be sure of its truth, there is much evidence to suggest that ancient peoples saw the moon as an indicator of fertility, and through observation of its link with menstruation may have developed lunar calendars, the evocative remains of which are carved into stone, bone, or horn. The very name for menstruation itself derives from the Latin *mensis,* or month. Modern witchcraft/Wicca sees the stages of the moon's monthly cycle as being linked with the Maiden, Mother, and Crone phases of the Goddess, and it is thought that our remote ancestors also viewed the moon as an outward manifestation of the Great Goddess and her journey from a young girl to a fertile woman, then to a hag, then back to a maid once more, though we have no absolute proof that this was so, and some of the myths surrounding the assumption may be wishful thinking or imaginative longing on the part of present-day pagans.

What we can be sure of is that many cultures throughout time have attributed womanly characteristics to the moon. The feminine, or yin, part of the Chinese yin-yang symbol may be lunar, and certainly symbolises gestation and nurturing; to the Mayans the moon was Ix Chel, the old goddess; to the Greeks she was Artemis the Maiden, or Selene, or Demeter of the full moon, or Hecate, who began her life as a goddess of the hearth, but was later a lunar deity of the Underworld and the crossroads, a crone; the Romans worshipped Diana, the counterpart of Artemis the hunter goddess. In tarot the moon is represented by the Priestess, the powerful and intuitive Maiden under whose feet the lunar crescent curves, and she rules over all that is instinctive, occult, and hidden. However, not all cultures have seen the moon as female. The moon was a god in Japan, Tsuki-Yoma, whose sister is Amerterasu, the solar goddess beloved of feminist witches. In India the moon is seen as having feminine characteristics, but yet the moon itself is a god rather than a goddess. The Sumerians saw the moon as a god as well: Sin, the son of the sky father Enlil and the earth mother Ninlil. In northern European traditions, the moon was male because it was seen as barren, cold, and cruel, whereas the sun—weak in the far north—was perceived as nurturing, nursing the crops into being with its gentle warmth.

What needs to be understood is that we project our symbolism on to the moon, thus personifying her in an attempt to relate to her and use her as an expression of our spiritual devotion. If we see the moon as Isis, or as Selene or Artemis, then the archetypal energies of our chosen goddess will reach us via the medium of the moon. Lunar energy is reflective and mediates whatever is projected upon it, whether that be sunlight (which is the light the moon receives and then reflects back to us from her larger, fiercer brother) or astral light. The magical energies of the moon form substance from the astral realm; the moon rules Yesod, the station on the Qabalistic Tree of Life that relates to illusion, but to psychic and spiritual power as well; and so we weave our magic, using the energies of a particular lunar phase to shape our intentions and give them an imaginative form that will manifest as reality on the earthly plane of being in due time.

In fact, within witchcraft and paganism, the many goddesses belong to the different points on the monthly lunar cycle, so that we may call on Demeter or Isis at the full moon, Hecate at the dark time, and Artemis when the first crescent appears inscribing her bow in the skies. There are, of course, many more goddesses whose attributes and personalities link them with the moon. The lunar rays are the bridge over which we cross to the place between the worlds where magic takes place. They are a channel for our devotion to the Goddess and for her love and blessings, and indeed for her presence within our rituals, where she may enter into participants in the sacred circle and uplift them, inspire them, mediate, and speak through them. We are all her priestesses and priests.

There are certain creatures that have always been associated with the moon, some of them across many countries and periods of history.

Modern witches know that the hare is an animal of the Goddess, a symbol of witchcraft and the lunar tides. But Chinese and Indian people alike also see a hare in the moon, which is said to be his home. In India people associate deer too with the moon god—the same beast who accompanies Artemis, and who is one form of the God to modern pagans. The toad is a witches' special creature as well, and he also lives in the moon according to ancient Chinese proverb. Another lunar animal is the bull, appearing in several cultures as a beast connected with a male moon deity, though he is linked with the sun also. At other times the bull is seen as sacred to the Goddess, to whom he might be sacrificed as a metaphor for the fullness and imminent waning of the moon.

People have observed the moon through powerful telescopes for centuries; men have walked on her surface; there are many statistics concerning her mass, her composition of minerals, her gravity, her size, and her orbit; yet none of these things has so far managed to destroy the mystery she holds for us or to make her any less magical or divine. The power she radiates can be understood symbolically or used with tangible effect in our rites and workings. Centuries of so-called civilisation have not diminished our instinctive responses to her waxing and waning and the power of her light in the nocturnal sky. We give praise to her and all she represents for us, just as our remote ancestors did when they gazed upon her face from the shelter of their cave dwellings. Sometimes we give her different names and qualities than the ones used in earlier times, but our response to her and our devotion have changed very little with the passage of history.

new moon

All is dark and still . . . but there is a sense of expectancy within that darkness, a stirring, a striving toward energy and growth; the forming of a tiny but brightly burning point of light. From the hush comes forth excitement; the shaping of fresh ideas; anticipation of the emergence into lighter nights when impulses quicken and creativity flourishes. Hecate withdraws, making way for the Maiden moon who will seize our thoughts and push us into outward activity once more. There is a spicy, piquant edge to our energy now. The tiredness and the drained feeling of the old moon have been replaced by an alertness that has yet to find structure and direction. Creative fire strives toward a goal that has not yet found expression. It is as if the moon's closeness to the sun results in a quenching of her light but also the honing of her impulse to bring creative ideas into form. We are faced with possibilities from which we have yet to choose.

Just as it's impossible to see a lighted match against the background of a blazing fire, so the glow of the moon is swamped by her proximity to the sun, which would normally give her radiance, and so when the moon is exactly new her dark face is turned toward us and she cannot be seen, even though we know she is there. In the same way, original and magical ideas that we may wish to bring forth and work upon in the fresh lunar cycle may not yet be illuminated; they are still in the realm of possibility, and may give only a glimpse of what they could later become. This is a still time, but that stillness is filled with tension; it is not tranquil or detached. There is a feeling of anticipation, of barely suppressed excitement, restlessness, and edginess, and an urge to be active and motivated, but a lack of direction in which to move. We sense that anything started now could short circuit, and yet we are impatient to get on with life. The moon's persona at this time is not necessarily gentle, as people who work with those who are violent or emotionally unstable will tell you; a surge of irrational behaviour often marks the new moon, though it may not peak as violently as at full moon.

Goddesses for this part of the moon's cycle are: Athena/Minerva, the Greco-Roman virgin goddess of wisdom, whose sacred bird, the owl, shows her connection with the Crone, whose phase has just ended; Artemis in her girlhood when she wandered wild and free, before she took on adult tasks such as midwifery; Persephone emerging renewed from Hades into the early springtime world; Inanna ascending toward the light again after her descent to the Underworld; Brighid, Irish goddess of poetry, healing, and smithcraft, whose festival is Imbolc, when the old is purified and the year's new ideas and goals first begin to emerge, and whose solar associations make her very apt for the time when moon and sun have conjoined to become the fiery forge on which potential ideas are hammered into recognisable shapes.

A MEDITATION FOR THE NEW MOON

Although it is of course possible to enact ritual at any time in the moon's cycle, the period just after the new moon lends itself more aptly to meditation and the forming of ideas that can be further developed once the crescent appears in the sky. Candles and incense are unnecessary, but if you especially want them, then use a small candle such as a miniature dinner candle or a birthday cake candle, and a fresh incense with a slight tang or spicy overtones—Isis is a good one.

Wait till dusk and then sit comfortably upright and alert some-where quiet and dark, such as the room you use for ritual, or in front of an altar or shrine. Be open to the energies of the moment; really let yourself experience the way the atmosphere around you seems to quicken, and yet takes you within. Observe closely how you feel. Consciously seek out the beat and rhythm of thoughts and feelings so that you are filled with an excitement that is irritable and restless as well. Take note of how this affects you, whether you experience it as exasperation or eagerness. Take some short, quick breaths in and out, tense the muscles all over your body, and then give a sudden shout. This should release the extra tension, allowing you to settle into the next stage of the meditation.

Relax and breathe deep into your belly, imagining as you do so that your whole being is opening out but taking you deeper within at one and the same time. This sounds a complete contradiction when written down, but try it and see how the experience unfolds for you. Sense darkness within, but realise that this darkness is not a total void; rather it is teeming with energy, potential, and creativity. Keep your breathing deep and regular, so that you seem to be inhaling and exhaling through your navel area . . . really attempt to feel your breath entering low in the body. Try to enter a state of listening awareness . . . you are listening for your thoughts, waiting for them to coalesce. If you have any ideas you had intended to develop or work toward in a magical sense in this lunar cycle, then allow them to focus as well, but don't force them, and be alert for fresh impulses too. As you breathe in, imagine that heat and power irradiate your being; as you breathe out, visualise a small bright point of light within the darkness, and watch it gradually grow, becoming stronger, clearer, and more con-centrated. Let the thoughts become focused too until you can sepa-rate them out and see what they are trying to tell you. Sometimes this kind of exercise, done before the moon is visible, can teach us a lot about our own impulses and creative drive, and ideas can emerge at this time that are more profound or more closely aligned with our deepest intuitive promptings. Of course, you don't have to do more than observe at this stage . . . just allow thoughts and impulses to show themselves and to wait for your input before unfolding their potential. Some thoughts will not be feasible, but some may be worth bringing into the light and incorporating into the magical work of the month ahead. Watch them all without judging until one or two particularly draw you: these may be the ones worth working with and expanding. Let your intuition guide you over their relevance and worth.

Finally, withdraw from the inner space and touch the ground to earth yourself, then think about what you have experienced, or write it down in your magical journal. Let its significance sink into your mind like seeds settling into the soil. In the next few days these seeds will take root and begin to grow toward the light, becoming visible with the moon's first appearance in her current cycle. If you like, you can take actual seeds and name each for a thought that inspires you and then plant them in a bowl of earth.

A goddess particularly relevant to this time is Brighid. Her activity spans both the very new moon and the time of the newly born crescent, leading from her smithing phase, when she brings thoughts and ideas into being from out of the flames of her forge, to her persona of poet when those ideas are shaped and given creative life. She is involved with the fire of smithcraft, the hearth fire, and the flame of inspiration necessary for any creative work. As the smith she is very much a solar deity whose sacred flame was kept perpetually alight by her priestesses, yet she is appropriate here because of the closeness of sun and moon at the start of the lunar round. The following is a prayer to her that can be recited to bring her help with fashioning reality from thoughts and aspirations:

> *Lady of inspiration, daughter of water and fire,*
> *Bright Goddess,*
>> *strike creative sparks from the anvil of my mind.*
> *Craft my desires from the metal of potential,*
>> *annealed in your sacred flame.*

Over the next two days or so, as the moon gains in strength, motivation increases, ideas settle into possibilities, and we gain the sense of direction that was difficult to find before. There is an upsurge of energy that is at the same time very grounded and purposeful. People seem to manifest a briskness and optimism as they go about their daily business, and it is possible to accomplish much more during the course of a day because life is flowing freely and accelerating into a much more outward and practical way of being. About two to three days after the point of astronomical newness, the finest silver crescent can be seen low on the horizon soon after sunset if the sky is clear. This is a potent time, when the energy is tender, bright, and uplifting, a time of purity when we can start work on fresh projects with the knowledge that the moon is now waxing and will lend her power to our efforts.

A white candle lit now and burned at dusk for a week will honour the Goddess and the new moon, and will send an atmosphere of peace, clarity, and purity into the environment. It is also lovely to cense the home with sandalwood, jasmine, or lavender incense, or maybe damiana. If the emergence of the lunar crescent falls on a cloudless night, then it is time to go outside, gaze on her, make a wish, or state whatever you want to bring into being magically, whilst enjoying the joyful lift she gives to the spirit.

The Goddess is still in her Maiden period, though growing through adolescence to young womanhood. Her character is airy, eager, and quick, and she can be appealed to for the vigour and enthusiasm to start something novel, or to carry an existing goal or project into a new phase. Following are several goddesses whose qualities make them appropriate for ritual work at this stage of lunar growth.

ARTEMIS

This Greek lunar goddess belongs to the entire stage from astrological inception to full moon, at which point she becomes the midwife to our realised dreams, though she is mainly called upon at the new moon. She is a fierce goddess, roaming the wild woods with her hounds behind her, bow in hand, a quiver of arrows slung over her shoulder and a deer by her side, and often accompanied by her band of nymphs. In Ancient Greece women led restricted lives, having a very circumscribed field of expression within the domestic and maternal spheres, and so Artemis represents an unusual aspect of Greek woman-hood, her autonomy and liberty being experienced only by young girls entering early adolescence, and these girls came under her protection. Those specially called to her service lived with a freedom seldom encountered amongst their peers within the strict society of their time. Dwelling in the forests, hunting for their own food, and learning self-sufficiency, they were known as the bear cubs of Artemis, for Artemis herself was thought of as a "she bear." She was the protector of animals as well, guarding them within her domain of mountains and forests, killing any mortal who threatened their safety. She is the twin sister of the sun god Apollo, the instinctual, feral counterpart to his rational, civilised, outward persona. But she may have her roots in a far earlier time than that of the Greek civilisation: she is an ancient goddess indeed, and her association with bears may go back to the Stone Age when these creatures were worshipped, their skulls placed in ritual positions within the darkest caves. As Artemis is so independent, it seems curious to find that she is also a goddess of midwifery and was beloved of pregnant mothers, but of course they and their newborn babies are also in need of her protection.

Artemis can be invoked when we need courage, independence, and the strength to venture out alone. She is not a nurturing goddess in the same sense as Isis or Demeter, yet she can be caring in her own way, and will fill us with determination and motivation if we call on her. Let her be a helper with the birth of creative ventures, the "children" of the heart and mind; or ask for her assistance during the gestation and birth of a real child. She is a special friend to women who have been down-trodden or abused by men, and consequently, as Diana her later Roman self, has been adopted by feminist branches of the Craft. Because Artemis is physically strong and active, she can aid in bringing the body back to fitness or building up athletic prowess too. She has a ruthless, cruel aspect that shows itself when those things dear to her are threatened, so be careful with wording in spells or invocations that call on her powers; make it clear that you wish harm to no one and that you intend to use her strength peaceably.

Here is an invocation to Artemis, which will call her energy into the circle at new moon rites:

> *Artemis run swiftly through the dusk,*
> > *where the hare bounds, there you are,*
> > *where the deer leaps your heart leaps too,*
> > *soaring to the open sky,*
> > *where the crescent of your bow curves bright and clear.*
> *Solitary huntress, keeper of the wild,*
> > *you are fierce, brave, and strong:*
> > *we need your courage.*
> *Draw back your bow,*
> > *release desire's arrows:*
> > *their target lies beyond this world.*
> *Be there to birth them when they've grown.*
> *They come to us from the realm of dreams.*

To summon Artemis into ritual, drum wildly but lightly, increasing the tempo, letting the drum beats patter like the racing feet of wild animals. Or chant quickly without words, building the sound into wild shrieks. If you are out in the open with plenty of room, then running in a circle or dancing freeform also raises the free, untamed energy of this goddess. Artemis is not a dainty, peaceful deity; she is a tomboy, a mixture of stormy adolescent and independent, self-motivated guardian and guide, so let your interaction with her respect her character. If you want someone to mother you or be patient while you sort out your feelings or direction, then you need one of the more maternal goddesses like Isis or Selene. But if you want the push to get up and get on, then Artemis will be a companion who motivates and supports you—as long as your needs run parallel with her interests.

Burn silver, white, or pale green candles for Artemis. Her sacred herb is artemisia or mugwort, and this can be smouldered in the form of moxa sticks from Chinese health shops.

INANNA

This goddess is very complex and needs to be understood before her essence can be worked with. She is the forerunner of the Egyptian Isis, the Babylonian Ishtar, and the Virgin Mary. This last is deeply interesting because there was a cult of sacred prostitution among Inanna's priestesses; so it is probable that the sexual side of Mary (unacceptable to the early church) was split off into the persona of Mary Magdalene, leaving the Mother of Christ shorn of sensuality. Astarte of Phoenicia and Canaan derives from Inanna too, as do Aphrodite and Venus. Inanna was the deity of the morning and evening star Venus, and her eight-pointed stellar emblem comes down to us via the tarot card of the Star. She had many other symbols as well, among them the lion, the cow, serpents, and the dove (this last image survived via Isis, Aphrodite, and Venus, and is still one of the symbols seen in some paintings of Mary). The crescent moon is one of her most powerful signs, showing her lineage as daughter of the Sumerian moon god Nanna. But Inanna rules over all the lunar phases, being a goddess of fertility, and the legend of her descent to the Underworld, from which she emerged after three days, shows her connection with the moon that is invisible for three days between the vanishing of the last sliver of waning moon and the advent of the thin new crescent; though it shows her association with the agricultural cycle too, her absence from the world causing the same barrenness as did that of Demeter when she abandoned the earth to search for Persephone.

Inanna's descent is a story rich in symbolism, and it was the foundation of later myths of descent and re-emergence, including that of Isis when she searched for Osiris, that of Persephone and Demeter, and probably even the death and resurrection of Jesus (who came forth from the dark tomb after three days). In the story, Inanna, Queen of Heaven and Earth, leaves her lover Damuzi and goes down into the Underworld to confront her sister Ereshkigal and claim rulership of this kingdom too. She passes through seven gates, at each of which she must leave some of her garments behind till she is naked. This imagery is a powerful metaphor for stripping away the layers of the ego, and also of moving through the occult seven levels of consciousness; but it was also the origin of the Dance of the Seven Veils, and is the basis of the *Legend of the Descent of the Goddess,* which comes at the end of Wiccan Second Degree Initiation, though Gardnerian Wicca attributes it to Aradia, who may very well be another successor of Inanna. When she finally reaches the deepest level, stripped bare of all protection, Inanna confronts Ereshkigal, who is both her sister and her darker self, and who might be seen as the Crone of the dark moon. Far from yielding to Inanna and handing over her kingdom, Ereshkigal hangs her sister's body on a stake, there to suffer the throes of painful death for three days.

With Inanna gone, the earth withers and crops die, and the light of the moon is absent. Inanna is permitted to be reborn into the upper world, but only if she can find someone to take her place. Upon returning she discovers that her lover, far from mourning her absence, has taken over her home, is sitting on her throne in her place, and is availing himself of her possession and having a wonderful time. She is understandably furious and decides he will be the one chosen to live in the Underworld in her stead. But with his own absence from the upper world, nothing grows anymore, for he is the grain itself and the life force of the growth cycle. Eventually he too is allowed to return to the world of light and to Inanna for half the year, during which time their union brings forth abundance; with the harvest he returns to the Underworld.

Inanna's symbolism and energies can be worked with through the entire moon's cycle, starting with the new moon, when she represents transformation and rebirth into the fresh cycle; continuing with the full moon and the harvesting of magical goals; and then with the waning moon, when she can aid in confronting anything that needs to be examined or released from our psyches. Call on her especially if the moon's new crescent coincides with your emergence from a time of loss or trauma and you want help to come to terms with what you have been through and wish to rise again from the ashes of the past and move forward with your life.

It is worth studying Inanna, for she is one of the oldest deities, and her symbolism and legends run like golden threads through the mythology and folklore of later cultures and can still be seen in some aspects of modern religious iconography. There is a large body of ancient hymns in her praise, which can be used as the basis for invocations to her, and which give many hints as to her personality and associations. These can be found through Internet resources and books on mythology.

The following is an invocation to bring her presence into your circle; it draws on some of the imagery and the titles given to Inanna by her original devotees; she was a goddess of war as well, but the intention here is to work with her fruitful and life-affirming qualities:

> Hail Bright Goddess, Daughter of the Moon, Queen of Heaven and
> Earth, Light of the World,
>> you wear the stars as your crown, the rainbow as your girdle,
>> and the earth as sandals on your feet.
> Lady of my hopes emerging from darkness again,
>> crescent moon and evening star,
>> you who are the beauty of the green world and the ripening grain,
>> whose harvest of wheat and bread, milk and fruit sustains me,
> Serpent Guardian of the Tree of Life,
> Holy Shepherdess, Lady of the Storm,
>> joy of my heart.
> Bless me with your presence tonight and always;
>> bring me the peace that you have won through pain,
>> heal my grief as yours was healed.
> Inanna, through your bounty I am renewed.

Inanna can be invoked by beating a tambourine lightly with the hand, chanting her name musically, or dancing gracefully and rhythmically. Burn an incense made of equal parts of frankincense and myrrh, with a quarter-part sandalwood and a quarter-part rose petals mixed with a few drops of pure vanilla essence or a sprinkling of ground or finely cut vanilla pods. Vanilla, of course, was not known in ancient Sumeria, having been brought from South America by the Spanish invaders, but it goes perfectly with Inanna's energies. Place an offering of any of the following on your altar for her: apples, grain, dates, figs, olives, or bread. In ancient times, bread was sometimes baked as a gift for her, made from barley, dates, and beer. Tightly budded white or pale pink roses can be put out too if they are in season. Light white, cream, pale pink, or pale yellow candles.

FREYA

Freya, whose name means "lady," is a Nordic triple goddess, the daughter of the sea god Njord and the twin sister of Frey. She is a goddess of love, in some ways like Aphrodite, but is also linked with death, being the leader of the warrior maidens, the Valkyries, and claiming for herself half the warriors who have died in battle. She is as fiercely proud and independent as Artemis. Also in common with Artemis, she is a goddess associated with animals: cats, swallows, and butterflies are sacred to her, and she is said to have the ability to shape-shift into a falcon, or to wear a cloak of falcon's feathers (shamans often wore feathered cloaks). Witches are attracted to her because of her reputation for sorcery and nocturnal magic. Her amber necklace, Brisingamen, is sometimes likened to the stars of the Milky Way. As mother to Balder the sun god, she has associations of sexuality and fertility, and she is especially connected with early spring.

Freya is a triple goddess of sexuality, birth, and death, but it is in her creative capacity that we can ask for her help at this time of the moon's round. Her special flowers are primroses and roses, and you can place an offering of honey in a bowl on the altar for her. When you invoke her, ask her for inspiration with imaginative work, or with developing qualities of courage and independence, or for commencing anything that requires an innovative approach or a surge of raw power.

Freya invocation:

Beautiful Lady with golden hair,
*   springtime flowers beneath your feet.*
Fly swiftly to me on falcon's wings,
Butterfly Maiden,
*   whose necklace is the stars;*
*   swallows dart before you;*
*   cats stalk your shadow,*
*   honey bees bring you their amber treasure,*
*   stolen from the rose's heart.*

There are many more deities who would be appropriate for the new moon. A visit to your local library or bookshop or some time spent online will yield a huge mass of information. Use your own judgment about which ones are best for your current needs, and listen to your intuition when invoking them or asking for their help; a lot of websites give distorted information, or their authors have twisted the essence of a goddess or god to suit their own conceptions so that the original persona is almost unrecognizable; it's best to study basic mythology first before investigating the way others have utilized the material. Some deities have a mixture of traits, so be very aware of these and take care to summon only their helpful and less argumentative characteristics. Don't be tempted to use their vengeful qualities to get back at someone else, as negative magic has a habit of backfiring on its creator—apart from which it just isn't nice!

It is fascinating to try to trace the characteristics that are shared by many goddesses. For example, Inanna, Isis, Aphrodite, Venus, Ishtar, Astarte, and Freya all have the rose as their flower. Freya and Artemis are both guardians of the animals. The dove has come down from the very earliest of times as a symbol of the Goddess, as have deer, cattle, snakes, and hares. These archetypal qualities have crossed the cultural divide and have survived through the thousands of years of global spiritual and religious history. You will find familiar traits cropping up again and again. The Goddess has many faces through which she can be approached or appealed to.

SOME MAGIC APPROPRIATE FOR THE NEW MOON

With each of these spells, you can ask for the blessings of a chosen deity according to which one fits your current needs, or you can simply ask for the help of the Goddess and/or God.

- Take a seed for each new goal, hold them one by one in cupped hands till you have thoroughly visualised each intention, then plant the seeds individually in a bowl of earth.

- Take a pure white candle, stroke it from base to centre and tip to centre with oil such as olive or almond. Be careful to avoid the wick or the candle will splatter when lit. As you dress it in this way, concentrate on a fresh new project that you wish to work on, then light the candle. Burn it every night at the same time till the moon is full.

- Invoke Artemis, then visualise yourself drawing back a bow and letting its arrow fly, carrying a wish with it to take root on the astral plane, to yield its harvest in due season. Really, really work hard at building up the image of your goal, and strongly picture the bow and arrow as well. It might help to see Artemis herself with bow pointing upward at arm's length, or see your own hands with the bow in them. Feel the strain and then the sense of release and hear the swish as the arrow arcs through the air. A visualisation like this might seem naïve and simplistic, but it can be extremely powerful—strong visualisation is the basis of most successful magic.

- Think of a goal, then tie three knots in a silver cord or ribbon, voicing your magical intention with each knot. Put it on your shrine or tie it in the branches of a tree in the garden till just before the next new moon, then untie the knots and cleanse the cord through the elements so that it can be used again for future spells.

- Go outside when the new crescent moon is visible and make a wish (but don't tell anyone else till it comes true!).

- This is a spell you can use if you're feeling insecure about your appearance (as all of us do from time to time). Sit in a candlelit room on the first night of the visible new moon. Place a small, very clean, circular mirror in the bottom of a water-filled chalice or bowl. Gaze at your reflection in the mirror and take notice of your best qualities: for example, you may have beautiful skin or large, bright eyes. Try to see more things worth liking about yourself. Ask the Goddess to help you recognise your own special attraction. Each time you feel hopeless about how you look, or seem to notice a blemish or less attractive feature, swirl the water in the container, then look at yourself again when it settles, telling yourself you are beautiful and as of much worth as anyone else. After two or three times you really will see yourself in a better light. Try it! When you've finished, drink some of the water, telling yourself that you are taking that confidence into yourself. Assure yourself firmly that your confidence will grow as the moon waxes.

- Hold three white budding flowers in your hands and verbally affirm three new goals with which you intend to work in this moon's cycle. Put the flowers in water on your altar or shrine and imagine that as the flowers open out, so will the potential held at the heart of each of your wishes unfold. Each day, go and look at the unfurling flowers and think about your magical goals. By the time they have fully opened, your aims will be well on the way to fulfilment.

BASIC NEW MOON RITUAL PATTERN

If you don't know how to cast a circle, then refer to the instructions in appendix A at the end of this book, which includes a step-by-step guide. The section in this chapter refers to the specific guidelines for this moon's phase. If you hold your ritual soon after dusk, then you will have the added bonus of being able to go outside afterward and look at the crescent moon if the sky is reasonably clear.

- Place white, cream, or pastel coloured budded flowers on the altar. Daffodils are wonderful in spring, and roses in summer.

- Burn white or pastel candles on the altar.

- Use damiana, lemongrass, lavender, or any other light, airy incense.

- Energy should be raised in a manner that is brisk or lighthearted: beating a bodhran or other drum with a quick rhythm would be perfect, or shaking a gourd rattle or rainstick.

- Call on a suitable goddess such as the ones mentioned earlier, or just summon the Goddess as Maiden. I've found she will arrive without much effort on the part of the celebrants, and will have an uplifting and tangible presence.

- Magic for the new moon should be concerned with fresh wishes and goals, or new stages in projects already underway. Work toward putting energy into starting each project, but ask for some staying power to prevent things from petering out again.

- For the feast, have light coloured foods such as shortbread or crescent mooncakes, and drink white grape juice, wine, or spring water.

Over the next few days, as the moon's crescent grows fuller, the general pace will settle to a steadier cadence. The airy, mental tempo of the very new moon will stabilise, but at the same time emotions will come more to the fore. Eventually a point is reached when the energies seem to pause briefly, while still holding a sense of excitement and optimism. The end of the new moon phase has been reached and the waxing phase is well under way.

eclipses

On August 11, 1999, I stood in my front room alternately watching the televised pictures of the eclipse from Cornwall and peering outside as the sky slowly darkened to an eerie, surreal dusk. Because totality happened in Cornwall about eighteen minutes before its maximum effect in Oxford, I was able to watch Saint Michael's Mount vanish into darkness, and then go out into the garden to watch the sky deepen to rich, evening blue in the middle of the day. This was the first total eclipse of the sun visible in Britain for seventy years, and even though it was less than absolute in Oxford at 95 percent, it was still a startling and intense event.

Eclipses have a reputation for being terrifying or destructive, but this was not my experience. I was aware of a profound feeling of inner initiation during the eclipse period. The day before there was the sense of a very deep, dark, positive serpent/earth energy. I awoke with a mood of great excitement on the morning of the eclipse itself. During the moment of totality in Cornwall, I lit a candle, a sacred act to express my commitment to the Goddess and God, who were conjoined at that instant through the medium of the sun and moon. I asked for peace and healing for the world, and for growth and healing in my own life. I remember that I was moved to tears and yet felt a depth of emotion that went beyond superficial sentiment and left me opened on an unfathomable level. This was partly due to the beauty of the television footage with the awesome pictures of the moments of total eclipse and the obvious emotion of those sharing in the event from Cornwall itself, but, even more, it was caused by the unexplainable spirituality of the occasion.

During this time the house was getting so dark that it was difficult to find my way around. Outside I sat on the bench in the garden as clouds swallowed much of the remaining light. It was extraordinarily quiet, no sound of bird song and no voices from other people either— I felt alone in the universe for a few minutes. My overwhelming and enduring memory is of remarkable peace and hush, and yet that peace was alive, not tranquil, and was deep beyond anything that I have experienced outside of meditation. Comparing my experiences afterward, I discovered that others had felt as I had, and many people considered that they had gone through something transformational. A few had been very lonely at the time of totality, some had been confronted by painful issues from the past, but not one had been unmoved.

My other close observation of an eclipse was on January 9, 2001, when the whole of Britain was given the opportunity to observe a total eclipse of the moon. My husband and I were able to watch approximately two-thirds of the moon being slowly eaten up by darkness before the sky clouded over. In contrast to my serene experience of the 1999 solar eclipse, I had felt very edgy for two or so days before, as though trapped by something beyond my understanding. When the earth's shadow fell across the moon, I felt such a sense of peace . . . as if the many "voices" I'm aware of all the time were stilled. It was wonderful. The sky cleared again in time for us to go out in the garden and see a bright crescent begin to form on the left-hand edge of the moon's disk, which itself was a deep brownish-red, like tarnished copper. It was quite lovely outside, really cold and frosty, with the moon showing between the trees, and the sound of next door's wind chimes in the holly tree; I was more intensely aware of such things than would normally have been the case. Despite the clouds that drifted across her face from time to time, we were treated to the awesome sight of the Goddess moving through all of her phases at an accelerated pace. The most remarkable experience visually was that of seeing her waxing from the left, the lunar sickle normally given to the Crone. My experience, and that of others I spoke to about it, was of something going out of me, leaving me feeling at peace and completely relaxed. I can only attribute this to the blocking by the earth of the moon's psychic force. It was an overwhelmingly beautiful event.

WHAT ARE ECLIPSES?

Eclipses occur when sun, moon, and earth line up in a specific pattern. Solar and lunar eclipses always happen within two weeks of each other.

Solar Eclipse

Solar eclipses can only happen at the new moon, when the moon actually comes between earth and sun, casting its shadow on the earth. This moon shadow has two parts, the dense inner umbral shadow and the progressively fainter outer penumbral shadow. Places on earth that the umbra touches will see a total eclipse, while those under the penumbra will see a partial eclipse. The entire eclipse sequence of totality for a specific place takes only minutes, though the buildup is considerably longer. The moon begins to pass over the sun from west to east, eating away the sun's disk bit by bit. Just before the eclipse reaches totality, the effect known as "Bailey's Beads" happens, a crescent of bright points of light caused by the radiance of the last visible portion of the sun striking the irregular edge of the moon. This is followed by the "Diamond Ring," so-called because the last points of the sun's light strike out in piercing white rays round the moon's perimeter. During the minutes of totality the flaring corona of the sun's atmosphere may become visible as well. At totality the sky is dark enough for some stars to appear, and wildlife may begin to settle into nocturnal behaviour, with birds roosting. It will feel suddenly cold.

The moon's shadow sweeps across the earth incredibly fast, so the total eclipse is soon over, and the sun gradually emerges again. The inner shadow of the moon is only about a hundred miles wide and is called the "Path of Totality," and any region outside of this will see less than a total eclipse, with the degree of darkness decreasing toward the outer edges of the penumbra. Only people living in the parts of the world where the moon's shadow touches will see a solar eclipse. If the moon is at its farthest from the earth, then an annular eclipse occurs, when only the centre of the sun is obscured.

A word is needed here about safety when watching a solar eclipse. The only safe time to look directly at the sun is during totality. If even a tiny portion of the sun, other than its corona, is visible, then it will be bright enough to damage the retina of the eye. This damage will be painless and may not become apparent till hours or even days after the event, and it will almost certainly be permanent. People have become totally blind after watching an eclipse with the naked eye. Pieces of glass darkened by being burned in a candle's flame are not sufficient protection, nor are sunglasses. Even the safety goggles sold for eclipse watching may not provide enough of a barrier to the sun's damaging light. Furthermore, the moments after totality, when the pupils of the eyes have been dilated to compensate for darkness, are the most dangerous, as the returning rays can more easily strike the inner eye. The best way to watch a solar eclipse is on television, or by casting its image on to a card through a pinhole cut in another piece of card. Remember, people have lost their sight entirely by watching a solar eclipse with unprotected or insufficiently protected eyes; any damage will not be felt at the time, but beware if you begin to see speckles or colours, and your vision fades to a lesser or greater degree.

Lunar Eclipse

Lunar eclipses take place on those full (or just past full) moons when the earth is lined up directly between the moon and sun and so casts its shadow on the moon; the portion of greatest shadow is the umbra, and that of lesser shadow the penumbra. A total eclipse happens if the three bodies line up exactly, but if the moon is slightly out of sequence with earth and sun, then the eclipse will be partial. Unlike solar eclipses, when only those in the path of the moon's shadow will be able to see the event, eclipses of the moon can be seen by anyone observing a sufficiently clear night sky at the time. The moon is not completely dark during its eclipse and will often glow with a reddish hue because the earth's atmosphere bends the sun's light, partially scattering the other colours of the spectrum, especially blue, and leaving red predominant. Lunar eclipses take longer than their solar counterparts, often several hours for the whole eclipse, with totality lasting roughly an hour. During the full sequence the earth's shadow reduces the visible moon to a slowly diminishing crescent. Lunar eclipses occur approximately every six months.

THE MYTHOLOGY OF ECLIPSES

The word "eclipse" derives from the Greek word for "abandonment," because to ancient people the light of sun or moon really did seem to have abandoned them. To our earliest ancestors who had no scientific knowledge and who therefore had no way of knowing that the light so suddenly engulfed would as quickly return, the natural phenomena of an eclipse must have been utterly terrifying . . . especially one happening during the day. Hundreds of years ago people thought that the sudden blotting out of the light of sun or moon presaged some disaster to their tribe or nation, or possibly foretold the death or downfall of a ruler or sovereign. By late Babylonian times astrologers were able to predict eclipses with great accuracy, and became responsible for warning the priests and rulers so that prepatory measures could be taken to avert the feared famine, war, or other disaster the eclipse was expected to cause.

From earliest times, eclipses have inspired a variety of myths, legends, and symbolism as people have attempted to understand the celestial phenomena taking place in the sky above them. To a wide spectrum of cultures, the event of an eclipse was personified as a demon or some other creature, very often a serpent or dragon, which was devouring the sun or moon—though to some races the beast was a wolf, a dog, a frog, or a catlike animal. Even modern astrologers call the moon's nodes, the mathematical points on the ecliptic concerned with eclipses, the "Dragon's Head" and the "Dragon's Tail." In ancient China, people would drum or shout or shoot arrows into the air to scare the creature away and free the sun during solar eclipses. The Romans too made a large amount of noise to scare away the demons they thought were devouring the celestial bodies.

To this day, some people in India will bathe in the Ganges during an eclipse, give charity, and perform other acts of religious devotion to ward off adverse effects. They hope that their attempts at propitiation will deter the demon attempting to swallow the luminaries; his two halves as Rahu (the head) and Ketu (the tail) represent the north and south lunar nodes and were once believed to be one creature. It is also widely held there that pregnant women must not see the sun or moon during the time of an eclipse for fear that their child may be born blind or with some other severe physical handicap. Any wounds such as cuts or insect and animal bites could be potentially lethal as well. The idea of eclipses bringing some sort of disaster has endured through the centuries.

All this is in complete contrast to the concept of the present-day pagan and New Age communities. Their belief is that eclipses are spiritual happenings that open a gateway to higher levels of being and give humanity, individually or collectively, according to other factors at the time of the eclipse, a chance to evolve spiritually or to come to terms with and move on from the psychological and emotional ties of the past. The union of sun and moon is now regarded as a sacred marriage rather than a dangerous confluence portending disaster, and pagans of various persuasions are vocal in relaying this information, which is becoming fairly widely accepted (witness the celebrations from Cornwall during the 1999 solar eclipse, when witches and other pagans figured largely in the media coverage). The public at large has embraced the wonder of eclipses too, and many people spend time travelling the world to be at the point of totality when solar eclipses occur . . . a whole branch of tourism has grown up around this. It seems that mythology has shifted to come into line with the changes in global society, and what was once a source of terror now fills many of us with a sense of magic.

THE DEEPER SIGNIFICANCE OF ECLIPSES

I love eclipses, which to me seem to have a very special and potent inward energy that, when worked with in a positive fashion, can bring creative transformation into one's life. I think they are a little like the dark moon energy, which can be used for inner transformation—the confrontation with the dark, devouring Mother, the Hag, which can help us release old conditions that are blocking our progress—in that they take us into the part of ourselves that is usually difficult to access due to the pace and "noise" of the way we live. However, eclipse energy is calmer and more magical than that. The amazing thing is that an event that lasts for such a short time can have enormously far reaching effects on the psyche.

Many sources advise that events related to eclipses are not immediate but unfold over the months before and after the actual astronomical happening. This may be true in the sense that the changes triggered continue for some time; however, it has been my personal experience that opening to and working with the energies of an eclipse will accelerate its dynamic impact on one's life, and that emotional, psychic, and psychological effects are apparent straightaway and to a profound degree. It could be that our changed perception of the meanings and effects of eclipses has resulted in a more eager absorption of their lessons so that the fear factor, which was a huge part of peoples' reactions to them in past ages, no longer holds us back.

Here is what fellow author and astrologer Leah Whitehorse had to say in an e-mail discussion about the January 9, 2001 lunar eclipse:

> I see the eclipse as the 4th hidden face of the Goddess—like dark Moon. However, I don't feel like I have got to grips with this just yet. There is a difference in an eclipse. Astrologically I see the eclipse as showing us our own shadows on an emotional level—perhaps rather a literal interpretation. To see our own shadow

can be very frightening yet also give us perspective as well. For a moment only darkness reigns but light soon returns. It always feels like something vibrant and intensely spiritual is happening. Seeing the shadow of the Earth on the Moon reminds me of how small we are. Yet I also see an element of perfection here— how our Moon, Sun and Earth are placed exactly so we can experience the eclipse. It takes my breath away. Seeing that which is usually hidden is a theme here—yet we are actually seeing something revealed by shadow. Maybe there is something to be said about what our own darkest elements can teach us about ourselves. At that moment when the Moon is totally dark our physical self may feel divorced from our emotional self, yet I always feel a tremendous surge of energy, but it borders on feeling chaotic. I can already feel the energy tingling in my body. Anyway—like I say—I'm still trying to work it out! I have never worked any magic on an eclipse—like I don't work on the dark Moon. That isn't to say I feel it shouldn't be done—I just feel like I need to be clearer on how I feel first!

At solar eclipses, when Goddess and God are conjoined, the temporary calming of the sun's force allows us to access our deeper selves without the interference of the dynamic, outward daytime energies we are usually subjected to. That is why there is such a sense of peace during totality. It is as though the God relinquishes himself in his surrender to the Goddess. Everything active or combative or hasty is stilled and we are released from the tension of our worldly selves. At some fundamental level we are given the opportunity to merge with the collective and pledge our future energies to work for the common good. Conversely, at an eclipse of the moon, the earth actually intercepts the tremendous psychic power of the full moon. The constant etheric chatter that normally bombards us, even if we are unaware of it, becomes silent and we are conscious of only our own thoughts and feelings and impulses, divorced from those of the myriad other beings with which we share our universe. If we can be open and honest with ourselves, this earthing process gives us a chance to look deep inside and confront who we are as individuals without having to take in the wider equation of our interaction with others and their impact on us. It is a chance to let go, to literally offer up what has been and move on, freed of the issues that are ours alone and that we no longer need.

During the actual sequence of an eclipse, it is better to simply watch and experience, possibly lighting a candle at the time of totality or soon after to pay homage to the deities and to celebrate the fresh start that is heralded by the return of the light. It's also good to meditate during the days leading up to an eclipse, when scattered or heightened emotions may be causing confusion, and this can have the effect of focusing intuitive attention on whatever the eclipse itself is likely to uncover. Visits to energy spots such as stone circles can powerfully tune one to the positive force of an approaching solar eclipse, while burial mounds with their inner, earthy energy can do the same for an eclipse of the moon.

I have found the following simple, short rituals to be very effective, the first to be performed the day before an eclipse and the second to be performed soon after the eclipse has ended, either the same day or a day or two later.

Pre-Eclipse Ritual

Cast a circle but don't use incense. The only candle is a black candle in the circle's centre, so there is no need to light point candles. Don't raise power. Sit comfortably and quietly and focus your attention inward, breathing steadily and deeply to still any restlessness and tension. Just allow yourself to unwind gently and gradually so that you can become aware of the deeper issues of your life, and what your spiritual self is trying to tell you about them. When you feel ready, and even if you don't think you have pinpointed anything worthy of note, light the black candle and say words similar to the following:

> *May this candle be the inner light, the hermit's lamp that guides*
> *me into my own darkness. May I have the courage to face whatever*

I find there, to understand, to let go of that which has no value for me now, and to move on for the benefit of myself and all those whose lives touch mine.

Be patient with yourself, and don't try to battle with issues that would be better talked out with a professional. The idea is to be aware of spiritual growth, not to force yourself to confront traumas that you have buried or put aside because they are too overwhelming to cope with alone. When you are ready, put out the candle and open the circle, then find something to eat and drink.

Post-Eclipse Ritual

Bring in a selection of food, drink, and flowers to celebrate the rebirth and transformation that the eclipse symbolises. Cast a normal circle with point candles, incense, and so on. If you like, you can put a number of extra white candles around the perimeter of the circle. Raise energy by drumming, chanting, or any other means that appeals to you and will lift the tempo. Call in the quarters and the deities, then light a separate white candle and say:

As the light has returned to the sky, so my path is illumined. I celebrate in the sure knowledge that I will see my way clearly in the days and weeks ahead.

Finish the ritual by feasting, singing, dancing, or anything else that helps you to enjoy the sense of liberation and wonder of the reborn sun or moon. Relight the candle every day for an hour or so until it has burned down.

THE NODES

A chapter about eclipses would not be complete without discussing the moon's nodes, which are intensely involved with eclipse patterns, being the two northern and southerly mathematical points where the moon's orbit around the earth crosses the ecliptic. This latter is the path the sun appears to take around the earth (the earth actually orbits the sun, but from our standpoint on its surface, the opposite seems to happen). The nodes form a pair of eternally linked opposites. They are so closely involved with eclipses because it is only when the new or full moon approaches within eighteen degrees of either node that an eclipse can take place.

Mythology of the Nodes

The information we have regarding the lunar nodes originally came via Hindu mythology, where the sun and moon are regarded as sacred, and eclipses therefore are seen as negative forces that temporarily block the luminaries. The tale is that long ago an elixir of immortality was obtained from the ocean and was offered to the planetary deities so that they would not die but could remain permanently in place in the solar system. While the gods waited to receive this divine nectar, a serpent or dragonlike demon disguised himself and so was able to take a drink. The sun and the moon realised what had happened and warned the god Vishnu, who severed the demon's head. However, the elixir had already been ingested and so the demon could not be killed. Instead his disconnected halves became Rahu, his head, and Ketu, his tail. To this day he lurks on the path of the ecliptic, trying to get his revenge on the sun and moon for denouncing him, swallowing them from time to time when they come close to him. Because the sun and moon are immortal too, they always come back to life.

The Nodes in Astrology

Most Westerners who have heard of the moon's nodes at all will have done so via astrology, where they are closely associated with the theory of reincarnation. In Western astrology, the north node is said to represent the path of the future, the direction in which we should be aiming, and the skills we should develop in our current life. Reaching toward the north node brings happiness and satisfaction. The south node is the place we have come from, the point where we have overdone or overreached so that pursuing its qualities now will bring dissatisfaction and problems. The north node has a flavour of Jupiter and the south node is likened to Saturn.

The viewpoint of Indian or Vedic astrology is somewhat different. The nodes are seen as shadow planets because they have no real substance but are simply mathematically defined points in space. Nonetheless, they are considered to be the repositories of extremely potent energies, and are, as in Western astrology, concerned with karma. Both nodes, however, are thought of as negative in some ways because they are capable of temporarily consuming the light of the sun and moon—though by the act of doing so they allow insight into the parts of our natures that are normally hidden. Rahu, or the north node, is likened in the chart to Saturn and can bring us worldly benefits, though may deny us any satisfaction in them. Ketu, the south node, is Mars-like and shows the karma we have brought with us, but also our past life talents. Unlike its Western counterpart, Vedic astrology encourages working with the south node, as it is an astrological point deeply concerned with spiritual wisdom and realisation. The aim is to integrate the two nodes so that both spiritual and material can work in a balanced and harmonious way, though to do this we have to confront the issues thrown up by both nodes. Although either node can be involved with either type of eclipse, traditionally Rahu is connected with lunar eclipses and Ketu with those of the sun.

Both systems see eclipses as opportunities for growth. However, the approach is somewhat different with each. In the West the current trend is to see eclipses as rather wonderful events that give a mystical glimpse into our deeper natures. The Eastern view supports the idea of seeing into our inner selves as well, but considers that the growth involved comes through recognising our darker selves and coming to understand ourselves through transcending the difficulties and pain involved in the confrontation, thus growing toward realisation of our higher natures.

Whether we take a negative view of the actions of eclipses, see them as marvellous and magical happenings, or adopt a purely scientific attitude, there is no doubt that they are fascinating and awe-inspiring cosmic events that have evoked a response from people since the beginning of time.

the first quarter

The sense of newness and purity are left behind, and the nocturnal skies are filled with radiance as the slender curve of Artemis's bow broadens night by night and the lunar crescent waxes. A feeling of purpose and motivation prevails and it seems much easier to get things done. People are more cheerful and relaxed in a way, but enthusiastic for enjoyment, activity, partying. Then, in the middle of this upward surge, it is as though everything stops, though this is hard to pinpoint or even notice immediately because it happens very quietly. It is just as though the world has taken a deep indrawn breath and paused. This pause is not necessarily tranquil, and it is certainly not stagnant—zest and excitement are waiting beneath its surface to unfold. Yet there is a feeling of balance held in tension as the moon stands poised to open into fullness. In the late afternoon and early evening she can be seen as an exact half, her face lit on the right, her left side in darkness, the glowing white of the dividing edge pared thin and crumbling like cheese cut with a serrated knife. The midpoint between new and full moon has been reached.

The first quarter *is* a time of balance, dynamic balance in fact, but it is fleeting. Once the dark half of the moon begins to fill out, the moment will have passed and energies will quicken again, picking up tension and momentum as the full moon approaches. But this brief pause is one of the most enchanted stages in the moon's cycle, and it can be used in a positive way to help magical goals along or to breathe some accord into relationships, both with oneself and with others. Work done now on integrating different sides of the self, such as body and spirit or mind and emotions. will be extremely effective and will lead to greater self-acceptance and self-worth. Similarly, working magically with a partner to increase cooperation and empathy will also be easier now than at other times in the lunar cycle. The analogy of balance between light and dark is made symbolically obvious if we glance at the sky and see the half moon hanging there. We may become aware that through integration we need no longer be torn apart by this and that, either or, but can have both, with neither assuming a dominant nor, conversely, a repressed role. This may sound very idealistic, but at first quarter there is a chance to realise some of these ideals.

However, first quarter is also a very good time to infuse extra power into the magical projects begun at the new moon. If extra effort can be directed toward this purpose, then a satisfactory result is even more likely. The other factor that may reveal itself is that of the workability of some of our goals. If something is unlikely to succeed, then that may become apparent now, if we take the time to listen and observe. A quiet turning in of focus, maybe while infusing power into a spell in progress, may nudge us into altering something . . . there may simply be a gut feeling that the emphasis needs to shift slightly for a project to be really effective. Similarly, a solution might suddenly present itself for an ongoing problem, or we may all of a sudden realise what is causing friction between ourselves and a partner, friend, or relative. There may be conflict beneath the outward signs of harmony right now that could be released and resolved.

Goddesses with whom it might be appropriate to work at first quarter are Aphrodite, Venus, and Kwan Yin. The first of these represents personal integration and balance, the second agreement in relationships, and the third universal compassion and harmony.

APHRODITE

Although Aphrodite is a Greek goddess, she has her origins in Inanna, Astarte, Isis, and the other goddesses who have evolved in this particular lineage. She is the goddess of love and sexuality, but also of self-esteem and self-regard, and so can be invoked when we wish to feel better about ourselves, especially over our appearance or attractiveness, or if we need to be more accepting of the light and dark halves of ourselves and the need to integrate rather than repress the latter.

Aphrodite was born of the foam that arose when Kronus castrated Uranus and threw his genitals into the sea. The west wind placed her on a seashell and carried her to Cyprus, where she stepped ashore at Paphos. She is the daughter of both sky and sea, and so blends airy and watery qualities in her personality as is shown by her romantic nature but also the detachment with which she viewed her relationships, always moving on when she grew tired of a lover. Aphrodite was so beautiful and so alluring to men that Zeus had her married to the old, lame smith god Hephaestus, who was meant to be a steadying influence on her. Unfortunately Hephaestus was totally smitten with Aphrodite and spent his time making jewellery and other adornments for her, including a magic girdle that made her even more alluring as far as males were concerned. She didn't remain faithful to Hephaestus, but had numerous affairs. The love of her life was Ares, the god of war to whom she bore several children. Another of her loves was the beautiful youth Adonis, who lost his life due to the jealousy of Ares. Aphrodite was responsible for causing quite a bit of conflict, and this side of her needs to be played down when appealing to her for help. Once a year the goddess would return to the sea and bathe, thus replenishing her youth and beauty. Her name means "born of the foam."

The value of working with Aphrodite at this part of the moon's cycle is that she represents the emergence of the Goddess from girlhood to womanhood, where she has matured sexually but is still independent of responsibility. She is able to maintain her autonomy within relationships, and therefore can help us to manifest self-respect and self-love, without which it is impossible to reach out to others on an equal footing. We can appeal to her to help with integrating and balancing the opposite sides of the personality so that we become more accepting of our faults, dealing with them without giving them more weight than they really have.

Put out roses or other opulent flowers, burn rose or vanilla joss sticks or incense cones, or good quality sandalwood chippings on a charcoal block. Pink candles are appropriate for Aphrodite, though avoid the deeper tones, as they are too passionate for this phase of the moon. It's important to be very specific that what you want is to balance your relationship with yourself, resulting in feelings of self-appreciation and self-worth. These are qualities that our current world age and society teaches are egotistical and undesirable, with the result that many people are driven to achieve in a career sense while devaluing their own attractiveness and humanity. It's okay for us to appreciate ourselves and allow ourselves a fair modicum of worldly pleasure and enjoyment, and bringing Aphrodite's voluptuous colours and scents into ritual space will open us to the joy that relaxation and self-indulgence can convey.

Speak simply to Aphrodite in your own words, asking her to help you become more accepting of yourself so that you can deal with your own shortcomings without being overwhelmed by self-blame or guilt. Resolve to deal with the aspects of yourself that you don't like, but also to appreciate your good qualities. Tell yourself you are a worthwhile person who has sometimes erred. Now ask for the space to relax and enjoy life, cosseting and pampering yourself from time to time. Lastly, imagine how much better your relationships with others would be if you brought this sense of relaxation and happiness to your encounters. When we are happy, then we let a lot of hurts and slights go by without minding too much. Becoming more inwardly relaxed, contented, and self-confident helps us to relate in a more harmonious way within our relationships with other people too.

Afterward, indulge yourself in some way. Have a relaxing, scented bath, and eat a box of chocolates or some other delicious food.

VENUS

Although Venus was based on her Greek counterpart, the stem on to which the Roman goddess of love was grafted had its roots in a far earlier time, with an agricultural goddess who was associated with vineyards, orchards, gardens, and spring fertility rites during which she was the Maiden of Flowers. Although her myth closely follows that of Aphrodite, with Vulcan being substituted for Hephaestus and Mars for Ares, she has a gentler and less selfish energy. In contrast to the more lusty Aphrodite, Venus became the keeper of chastity for women, and the initiator of marriage and the guardian of marital fidelity in women (reflecting the Roman attitude toward females, which was more repressive even than the Greek). Her realm is that of both personal and spiritual love, where she promotes harmony and happiness. Like Aphrodite, Venus was born from the sea. She has given her name to the morning/evening star, which was Inanna's emblem.

As with Aphrodite, Venus can be invoked with the aid of rose, sandalwood, or vanilla incenses, and roses in bloom. All paler shades of pink candles are appropriate, as are mauve, blue, apricot, and pastel green. When you have created a harmonious and fragrant atmosphere, ask Venus to help you with your own part in any relationships that have hit a stormy patch, or within which there may be misunderstanding and tension. When asked, she can help us to restore equilibrium by showing us how to smooth our own ruffled feelings and be more loving and forgiving.

KWAN YIN

Kwan Yin stands or sits on a lotus flower. Sometimes she is seen holding out one hand, and sometimes she is many-armed, the hands holding the different gifts she brings to us. The origins of this Asian goddess are somewhat tangled and obscure. It is probable that she is an amalgam of an original Chinese goddess and the feminisation of the Buddhist male saviour or spreader of compassion, Avelokitishvara, who was known as Chenreizig in Tibet. She may also incorporate aspects of the Tibetan Tara, a female deity also concerned with compassion. Deities are related to on two levels in Buddhist culture, one in a literal sense by people who wish to appeal to them for help or advice, and the other in a symbolic sense within monastic practice, where the basic concept of theism is not accepted and gods and goddesses are perceived as symbols for qualities practitioners may wish to incorporate into their lives. It is in the former sense that she is beloved of many thousands of people throughout the Far East, including in Bali, Vietnam, and Japan.

There seems little doubt that Kwan Yin is an aspect of the Great Goddess. She is sometimes seen carrying a sheaf of rice, like the Western sheaf of corn, or pouring out the waters of life and healing. She is also deeply involved with fertility and childbirth, and is appealed to by women wishing to conceive. She represents serenity, healing, mercy, and peace, and manifests many of the qualities of the Virgin Mary or Isis. It is said that Kwan Yin hears the cries of all beings. Having a picture of Kwan Yin in your home or a statue of her on a shrine or altar will bring a tangible sense of peace and hope into the environment.

Light a candle for Kwan Yin at this moon phase and open yourself to the concept of love for all of creation. Concentrate on feelings of serenity and compassion. Ask Kwan Yin to bring those qualities into your own life. Try to spend a little time visualising love spreading out from your heart into the world, so that it can be sent to where it is needed most. See the loving energy like rays of light radiating from your heart chakra; actually feel the caring, healing power. Buddhists have a concept that they call "Metta," and this is loving kindness toward all beings . . . even those people whom we dislike or with whom we have had experiences of conflict. Attempting to send loving kindness to everyone, regardless of whether we like them or hate them, can bring peace, acceptance, and a love and understanding of ourselves and everything else. Don't specify individuals to whom this healing power is to be directed, but instead send it out widely and universally so that your thoughts encompass the whole world—every person, creature, rock, and blade of grass.

WORKING WITH FIRST QUARTER ENERGIES

It's perfectly okay to work ritual on this part of the moon's cycle, but often it's better to use the special power it brings to review work already in progress, or to gain insights into the way spells are unfolding. If you are lighting a spell candle daily, pause in the process of igniting the wick and tune in to how the spell is forming. Does the energy feel right? Do any new factors occur to you that might improve the end result: for example, you may gain a sudden feeling about the way the goal should manifest, or some details may become clearer and would profit from added visualisation. Another beneficial use for the first quarter is to quietly go within in contemplation or meditation and see what needs to be done when the full moon arrives, what magic might be appropriate then, or which areas of your life could benefit from focus and attention.

The moon's quarters are not widely used in magic and ritual, and yet they are valuable stations on the cycle when loose ends can be tied up and impetus gathered before entering the next stage.

the man in the moon

Present-day pagans have chosen to attribute lunar qualities to the Goddess, and her cycle is intertwined with the phases of the moon, but as mentioned in earlier sections of this book, not all cultures or periods of history have viewed the moon as feminine, though many of those with male lunar deities thought of them as guarding or regulating female menstrual and reproductive cycles or natural growth phases. In the Near East there was a moon god on whom the Islamic Allah may have originally been based, just as their holy Ka'abah stone was once linked with the Goddess. To the Celts the moon was often a masculine deity, and to Nordic people also. My German friend has told me that she too was brought up to refer to the moon as male. The Chinese to this day still hold an autumn harvest festival for their moon god to whom they pray for fortune and happiness within the family. Mooncakes are made, and people go outside to gaze at the moon and ask for his blessings and protection. There are many instances of moon gods, some of whom are mentioned below.

TSUKI-YOMA

In the Shinto religion that predated Buddhism in Japan and exists alongside it in the present-day, the myth tells how Amerterasu the sun and her moon brother Tsuki–Yoma were born from the eyes of a great god. They lived happily together in the sky, until one day they quarrelled, after which Amerterasu took herself off to the opposite side of the sky, which is why the sun and the moon are never seen together.

ANNINGAN

In Inuit legend, Anningan is the moon god who lusts after his sister Malina the sun goddess and continually chases her across the sky. So intent is he on his lascivious pursuit that he doesn't stop to eat and so consequently grows thinner and thinner until he is no longer visible. At this point, overcome with hunger, he eats to make up for the days of deprivation and grows fatter again, till he is large and strong enough to begin the chase once more. Malina meanwhile keeps as far away from him as she possibly can, hiding behind the earth, which is why sun and moon rise and set at different times. Anningan's fluctuating weight is the explanation for the waxing and waning of the moon.

CHANDRA/SOMA

Chandra, or Soma, is the Hindu lunar god who is associated with the astrological moon. However, as Chandra he was the pre-Hindu lunar and fertility god on whom the present day Soma was originally based, and his nightly tears fall semenlike as life-bringing dew. His animal is the deer or antelope, and he drives his moon chariot across the sky pulled by ten white horses. The word "soma" refers to an elixir or magical drink that supposedly produces ecstasy and/or immortality, and so Soma himself may have links with hallucinogenic herbs, though the symbolic meaning of soma is that of the life force itself. Despite being governed by a male deity, however, the moon in Indian culture is seen as possessing traditionally feminine qualities such as nurturing, and represents the mother in astrology.

THOTH

Thoth has the body of a man and the head of an ibis, a bird sacred in Ancient Egypt, and he wears a lunar headdress incorporating both the crescent and full moons. He can often be seen carrying a crescent moon-shaped knife with which he is said to have slain the wicked. He was believed to have invented writing. Though he is often linked with Hermes and Mercury because of his skills with language, geometry, astronomy, medicine, drawing, and other hermetic attributes, and because he is sometimes seen holding writing implements, he was originally an Egyptian moon god. He was also a god of the Underworld, where he helped to weigh the hearts of the dead in the scales of Maat. The ape was sacred to him. He later became a god of wisdom and magical skills, and in this capacity he was associated with magic and alchemy during the medieval period.

KHENSU

This Egyptian moon god is sometimes seen as an aspect of Thoth and sometimes as a deity in his own right. However, it is likely that he is an extremely old god from the pre-Dynastic Nile Valley who was adopted by the later Egyptian people and absorbed into their pantheon. Like Thoth, he is distinguished by a moon disk and crescent moon emblems, and he too has links with writing. He is a young god, as can be seen by the lock of hair falling over his face, such as was worn only by male children in Ancient Egypt. Sometimes he is represented with a hawk's head. He is connected with fertility and growth in creatures and crops alike, and it was believed that during his crescent moon phase both women and livestock conceived. One legend tells that he lost some of his light to Thoth in a wager, and now has insufficient radiance and so is forced to wax and wane to conserve his power.

SIN/NANNA

Mesopotamian moon god Sin, or Nanna, was conceived when his father, the god Enlil, fell in love with and raped the goddess of air,

Ninlil. He was banished to the Underworld as punishment, but Ninlil, realising that she loved Enlil in return, followed him. So that their child, the moon, would not be trapped in darkness, the couple promised that they would leave their future children in the Underworld in his place, and so Nanna was born in the upper world, where he lights up the night.

Because the new moon crescent is like a bull's horns, Nanna was likened to a virile young bull, and was thought to rule over herds of livestock, particularly cattle, and to be a bringer of potency and fertility. Nanna is said to have brought humanity the idea of measurements of time because of his cyclic nature. From waxing to waning, Nanna sails the nighttime skies in a circular boat, but when the moon is dark it is because he has gone down into the Underworld to rest and to judge the souls of the dead. During his time above ground, he brings abundance and fertility to the land and initiates the conception of children. He fulfils, in fact, many of the functions expected of a moon goddess.

It is worth exploring the theory of a masculine moon, even if we choose not to pursue this notion within spiritual and ritual practice. Men may not menstruate or become pregnant, but that doesn't mean that they don't undergo hormonal and emotional changes through the course of a month, and they are as capable as women of conceptualising a goal and bringing it to birth. Lunar energy affects everything, from the tides to sleep patterns and plant growth, and these areas of life are certainly not necessarily gender biased. It might be worth asking how far our ideas about the sun and moon as archetypal symbols are based on the gender stereotypes of our culture. Do we see the sun as masculine because he appears to be fairly steady and constant, yet can be dominant, fiery, and aggressive, in keeping with our idealisation of masculine roles within the family and society in general? Do we equate feminine characteristics with the moon because we have been taught to regard women as emotional, fickle, and changeable? How far are these gender judgments really true? Are not women capable of great strength and dependability? And is it healthy for men to be expected to repress their emotionality and sensitivity, or their nurturing qualities? We need to be aware, too, of the extent to which people in all ages and cultures have perceived the luminaries in the light of their own climate, geographical features, and social values, or have projected their own needs on to them. Interestingly enough, as can be seen from many of the aforementioned legends, where the moon has been seen as male he has often exhibited stereotypical male characteristics, such as lust, pursuit, and gluttony, whilst still retaining the lunar qualities of nurturing and growth. However, some female lunar deities act in what is seen to be a masculine manner, as in the example of the hunter goddess Artemis, who exhibits many of the characteristics we tend to think of as male, such as independence, aggression, and cruelty. It would be an interesting experiment for both men and women to try to apply opposite gender traits to sun and moon, maybe as a meditation exercise. This could be of value to single-sex groups, as well, who wish to transpose the usually accepted qualities on to the opposite gender luminary.

full moon

The moment of balance at the first quarter has been left behind, and the nocturnal skies grow brighter so that even on cloudy nights there is a discernable glow. The moon moves through her gracefully curving gibbous state and sails majestically toward full. Excitement seems to vibrate in the air, filling the lungs and suffusing the body with each breath. There is an increase in jollity and high spirits so that people have more energy than they know what to do with, and some of this spills over into tension and conflict. Animals become more restless, more wilful—the idea of dogs baying at the moon is founded on a reality that is very apparent now—and even well-fed domestic cats want to be out hunting. Summer nights are redolent with the perfume of flowers, magical, exotic, and in the long evenings swallows fly late and bats, pursuing the same airborne insects, dip and flutter over field and garden. Winter nights acquire an extra crispness and clarity that bring intoxication to the blood and make one want to be outside despite the coldness.

At full moon, the point of maximum strength has been reached in terms of occult force and power. There is a buildup of extra etheric tension that can be uncomfortable if it isn't discharged through activity, whether that be dancing, partying, physical action, creative work, or magic. If you have crystals in your environment, you may notice that they are extremely active at this time, projecting a wide force field. Clairvoyance and other psychic abilities will be enhanced now for many of us. It is as though the full moon is a gateway to other realms of being, the energies of which flood on to our plane and interact with us. For many people, there is a sense of mystical longing that is almost unbearably poignant. The Goddess has entered the phase of the Mother and is pregnant with potential. Any work that was started at the new moon is nearing the time of harvest, or at least can be given a massive boost of magical power to move it to the next stage. Everything is ripening in an occult sense, moving to culmination, resolution, and possible release.

The best time for full moon magical activity is while the force is still building, up to and including the actual astronomical fullness. Though it is still useful to work after this time, the power will be imperceptibly ebbing, so is more appropriate for healing or for the resolution of spells already in process rather than for anything fresh. If you have a wish that needs one concentrated push to get it off the ground, then just prior to full moon really is ideal. It is very rare for this type of magic to fail if it is properly thought through and carried out. The optimum time then is the day before or the day of total fullness. The day after is still effective, but slightly less likely to yield success.

Goddesses for the full moon period are Selene the Greek lunar goddess; Greek Demeter, who is a triple goddess; Isis of ancient Egypt; Tuscan Aradia; Inanna in her more mature and fulsome aspect; Hindu Lakshmi; and the Celtic nature/lunar goddess Anu.

SELENE

Selene is the sister to Helios, the sun god, and like him she travels the sky in a horse-drawn chariot, though hers is silver and the journey is made at night, while his golden chariot traverses the daytime heavens. Selena is young and beautiful with a white face; she wears robes and has an expanded silver almost-half-moon crescent on her brow. Sometimes she holds a torch in her hand. Other times she rides a bull, link-ing her with the moon bull of earlier cultures. Selene had many lovers, but her true love was Endymion, a shepherd whom she discovered sleeping in a cave and whom she seduced. Together Selene and Endymion had many daughters. Eventually Selene, knowing that Endymion was mortal and that she would one day lose him to death, begged Zeus to allow Endymion to choose whether to become immortal and stay with her or to remain mortal. Endymion chose immortality but had to remain asleep in his cave, where he was visited nightly by Selene.

Selene is the full moon goddess most involved with romantic love. Burn white and deep pink candles for her and appeal to her to bring romance into your life, or to nurture an existing relationship. Be very careful with wording here. It is not ethical or appropriate to use magical means to try to make another person romantically interested in you if he isn't already. Be very wary as well if you are at all tempted to ask Selene to bestow immortality on your current relationship. You and your lover *may* be destined to be together through all eternity; on the other hand, you may grow apart and regret any bond that keeps you tied once the joy has gone out of the relationship.

Here is an invocation to Selene:

Gentle Lady with your glowing face,
moon upon your brow,
radiance all around you.
Shine down on me,
bring your beauty to my life,
bless me with love.
May my heart be glad.

ARADIA

Aradia supposedly comes from Italy, from the Tuscany region. There is some controversy surrounding her origins and whether or not she is a true part of Tuscan folklore. In the 1890s, a folklorist named Charles Leland met a young Italian woman, Madalena, who claimed to be a witch—more specifically, part of a hereditary group of witches called the Strega. She dictated a volume of material to Leland, including the legend of the goddess/saviouress Aradia, daughter of the moon goddess Diana, or Tana. Leland subsequently published Madalena's tales in the form of a book called *Aradia, The Gospel of the Witches.* There is some doubt as to the authenticity of the book, especially as Leland was not always respected as a particularly accurate researcher, being thought to be gullible and easily fooled. Indeed, it has been suggested that Madalena was making fun of Leland and invented the whole topic of Tuscan witches to lead him astray.

Whatever the truth behind Aradia's legend, she is one of the most popular deities among the Wiccan community, and Alexandrian Wicca in particular has adopted her. Doreen Valiente's beautiful and well known *Charge of the Goddess* was directly based on a similar charge in Leland's *Aradia,* and in various forms it is in widespread use throughout the global pagan community, with versions by Starhawk, Shan Jayran, and many other well-known witches being utilised within ritual work.

There are two versions of Aradia's story. In the first she was a real person who was born into a noble family but disguised herself as a peasant so that she could help the oppressed and the poor. In the second version, Aradia was the daughter of Diana the moon goddess and Lucifer the sun god. Aradia saw the terrible conditions in which the common people of Tuscany were living, and she came to earth to teach them and to help them escape from virtual slavery, showing them magical skills that could heal them and make their lives freer, counselling them to meet in groups when the moon was full. During this time some of the nobility became threatened by her activities and had her killed. Much like Jesus, her body was put in a cave, from which she emerged after three days alive and well to carry on her work among her followers. This latter part of the legend is in keeping with many other lunar myths in which a deity comes back from darkness or death, much as the moon becomes visible again after three days to begin a fresh cycle.

Aradia can be invoked as the sole goddess in a full moon rite. I have not written an invocation to her as there are so many already in circulation. "Drawing Down the Moon," the act of calling the energy of the Goddess into one of her priestesses, is often done after reciting one of the versions of *The Charge of the Goddess*.

INANNA

This Sumerian goddess is mentioned in the section of the book dealing with the new moon. The preparations for her can be used at full moon also. However, deep pink candles and red roses can be substituted for the paler colours of the earlier lunar phase. Inanna is a goddess concerned with love, fertility, and motherhood, and can be appealed to at the full moon to bring those qualities into the lives of anyone wanting to utilise her gifts. The following is a suitable invocation to her:

> *O Lady of the Animals,*
> *Radiant Goddess,*
> *Queen of Heaven and Earth,*
>   *you wear the stars about your head,*
>   *the moon as your crown.*
> *The rainbow is your garment as you walk the skies.*
> *You who ripen the grain and bring the cattle to birth,*
>   *bless our lives with riches and fertility.*
> *We give praise to you now and always.*

A small word of warning when working with or meditating on Inanna: she is a goddess deeply involved with sexuality, whose priestesses willingly gave of their bodies to men visiting her temples, and using her energies may increase your libido or bring sexual encounters into your life, so she is not a deity to work with if you are going through a period of voluntary celibacy.

Inanna Meditation

On the night of the full moon, burn incense chosen from the range appropriate for Inanna, which includes sandalwood, rose, and vanilla. Light white candles and then sit in their glow, preferably on a cushion on the floor if you can do so comfortably. Close your eyes and gradually let yourself relax, breathing deeply and gently but without forcing your breath in any way. Smell the incense, and see the candlelight seep golden through the reddishness of your closed eyelids. Imagine your everyday surroundings fading out, to be replaced by the rough walls of an ancient room, lit by reed lamps. You can feel an earthen floor beneath your feet, though rugs and hangings in dim, rich colours adorn the walls around you.

There is a doorway before you made of two tall bundles of reeds that arch over till their ends cross, and through this entrance you gain an impression of night sky washed with a faint radiance as though the moon is soon to rise. But as you bring your focus back to the archway itself, you can see that a change has taken place. The reeds have gone, replaced by stone carved with writhing, stylised serpents above whose heads a crescent, maybe the horns of some beast but somehow reminiscent of the new moon, cups an eight-pointed star. Something compels you to rise to your feet and walk through the stone exit, out into the warm night where the fragrance of roses and many other flowers scent the air.

You walk on, skin caressed by the breeze. The moon has risen fully now and its milky glow lights up a landscape opulent with fields of grain, sloping down to a river just visible as a silver curve between the rough trunks of date palms. The ground is clothed with grass and herbs that release the scent of basil, bruised by your passing feet. The ears of corn seem huge—dusky muted gold in the dreamlike luminosity, coarse and heavy to the touch as your hands brush against them. To right and left, here and there, fruit trees group into orchards laden with apricots, apples, and other ripe fruits whose gorgeous smell reaches you on the balmy air. There are cattle grazing near the trees. In the distance a lion gives voice briefly, a sleepy, muted cough, then is silent.

Soon you can feel the ground begin to rise so that you are walking up a gradually steepening slope. Above your head, high over the round disk of the moon, stellar constellations arch, their stars huge and bright, and you realise you are looking at the zodiacal band against which all life on earth is played out. The faint breeze has died away and the night is still and quiet except for the scuff and rustle as your bare toes crush the grass and pass on. Yet out of this peace a tension is forming, delicious and filled with portent. Your loins feel pleasantly heavy, but your footsteps are springing and energetic despite the incline up that you process. A sense of deepening bliss steals into your consciousness, filling you with wonderment and delight.

As you approach the top of the rise, twin cedars flank your route, branches meeting over your head to frame the burning lamps of stars, and the air around is redolent with a spicy, woody odour. As you pass beneath this second arch, you know that you are nearing the source of magic that has drawn you out into the night. The atmosphere is electric, exhilarating, and yet strangely calm, so that your limbs are tingling but your mind is peaceful, open to whatever lies ahead, yielding to a sense of inevitable surrender.

At last, before you is the heart of the mystery. On the crest of the hill grows an apple tree, its branches very even, and a bright crescent moon adorns the topmost twigs, made of some silvery metal that seems lit from within. Before the tree is a throne of stone or smooth wood, its arms carved into the forms of stylised lions. The throne's tall back culminates in a lion-headed bird with outstretched wings. On the throne a woman sits suckling a baby. She wears a flounced skirt, but her breasts are bared, and there is a horned crown nestled among the wild black curls that flame around her head. She is radiant, her aura emanating power, and you know instinctively that she is the source of the wonderment that has called you here. And yet she is earthy too, almost as though she is part of the landscape, not unapproachable at all. She has kicked off her sandals and her bare toes curl into the grass at her feet where ears of wheat grow by the edge of a lively brook. There are white lilies and tiny stars of jasmine threaded in the hair that tumbles at her shoulder, and their brightness draws your eye beyond to the double-headed axe resting against the throne, and beyond that still to where a white bull crops the grass under the apple tree, the chain by which he is tethered jingling faintly as he moves.

The child stirs in her arms and, as she shifts his tender weight, he turns his head to you and you can see the man he will become, hair so black, eyes intense, skin silken. As his eyes meet yours, there is the sounds of drumming hooves and a stag leaps across your field of vision, darts down the hillside, and is gone. The bull roars, horns wide and sharp as his head comes up, pulling against the chain that strains but holds. Then the child nestles into the breast once more, rooting for the nipple; the moment passes, all is calm again, but you are left with a strange presentiment you can't decipher.

Lifting her head and meeting your gaze at last, the woman beckons to you and gestures for you to sit at her feet, where milk and olives, dates and bread, and honey are laid out in flagons and containers on the ground. You eat and drink, hardly tasting anything because the pressure of her hand, gentle on your head, is sending such joy and yet such longing through and through you. The moonlight intensifies to dazzle your eyes so that you involuntarily shut them tightly. A sound— you cannot tell if it is music, or the voices of birds, or simply starsong from the depths of the heavens above you—rings through your ears. Pain and passion and sweetness mingle, drawing you out of yourself, away and away, spinning you into unfathomable depths yet higher than the clouds.

Again you are aware that a significant moment has passed. You feel alert and grounded again. You open your eyes and find yourself back in the building where the journey began. One by one blow out the lamps, close your eyes once more, and see the glow of candles begin to seep through your eyelids. Sense the return of familiar surroundings, the cushion under you, the floor of your room back in your everyday world. When you feel totally centred, open your eyes. Take some time to write down all you have experienced, then eat and drink.

ISIS

Isis is the archetypal Mother, the queen of all the goddesses of all time, the most popular female deity ever, having travelled from her native Egypt through the Near East to Greece and as far as Britain in Roman times, being one of the prime deities worked with by occult societies such as the Golden Dawn, being the basis for the Priestess and Empress tarot cards, and enduring into modern pagan and Wiccan rituals. She was based on Inanna and Ishtar, and gave rise to the appearance, characteristics, and symbolism (though in a much diluted form) of the Virgin Mary. She is the spirit of the universe, being seen in the starry heavens and at the heart of the natural world. Isis, known to the Ancient Egyptians as Aset, is lover, Mother, sister, wife, and queen. As Queen of the Heavens she wears deep, radiant blue. As the Queen of Nature she wears green and nurses her baby. In Egyptian times she wore a throned headdress because she *was* the throne itself on which the pharaohs were supposed to be supported. Later images of her show her wearing a horned crown on which rests a solar or lunar disk, and this symbolism shows her links with Hathor the cow goddess in later Egyptian dynasties. The red rose is her flower, showing her connection with the Sumerian and Babylonian goddesses who preceded her. Like them she went into the Underworld, and like them too she commands serpents and is the Lady of the Star—not, in her case, Venus, but the Dog Star Sirius, whom Egyptians thought responsible for the rising of the River Nile that overflowed the flood plains and made cultivation possible. She owns the swallow, the falcon, the kite or vulture, and the dove. Sometimes she is seen as winged, when she can enclose her children protectively. Usually she is a slim and graceful figure shown with her sister Nepthys, or seated on a throne suckling Horus, her son. No goddess in the whole of humanity's spiritual history has been so loved or revered or has so captured the imagination.

Isis and her husband Osiris were born from the same womb. They always loved each other. Osiris became the king of Egypt, but his jealous brother Set plotted to get rid of him, luring him into a casket he had made to trap Osiris, nailing down the lid and setting the wooden casket afloat on the Nile. From there it drifted out to sea and over the ocean, coming to rest at last entangled in the branches of a fragrant tree. The rulers of that country wanted the wood of the aromatic tree for a pillar to support the roof of their palace, and so it was cut down and built into a column with Osiris in his casket inside.

Meanwhile, the grief-stricken Isis had gone into mourning and searched the world for her lover. She came at last to the palace, disguised as a humble widow, and took the job of nursemaid to the queen's son. Perceiving special qualities in the child, Isis decided to make him immortal by gradually burning away his base qualities; but the queen saw what was happening and thought her son would die, so snatched him from the flames. At this, Isis revealed her divine nature and demanded that she be given the supporting pillar that contained Osiris in his box. Cutting away the tree trunk from around the casket, Isis removed the container and found a boat to take her and her husband back to Egypt. During the voyage she transformed herself into a kite and hovered protectively over her husband's body. During this time she also found the opportunity to conceive Horus with him.

When they got back to Egypt, Isis hid the casket in the marshes so that Set wouldn't find Osiris while she went off to care for her newborn son Horus. But Set found Osiris and dismembered his body, scattering the fourteen pieces the length and breadth of the country. The heartbroken Isis searched far and wide for Osiris's body parts, aided by her sister Nepthys and her son Anubis, the jackal-headed god who was also Osiris's son (he had lain with Nepthys when she had disguised herself as Isis in order to seduce him). Eventually Osiris was reassembled except for his penis, which had been swallowed by a fish. A false penis was made for him, and he was then embalmed and sent into the Underworld. Here Isis revived him with the wind from her beating wings and brought him back to life, and he became the judge of the souls of the dead.

Thus Isis and Osiris enacted the ancient vegetation theme of the Goddess and her dying mate, and their cycle was entwined with the fertility of the Nile Valley.

Isis is such a universal goddess that she can be called upon for help with almost anything you can think of. She is the Great Mother, the preserver of life, the bringer of healing and fertility, and her story incorporates all the lunar aspects, starting with her youthful Maiden phase, then her role as the Mother of Horus, and finally the Crone phase, both as the mourning widow in search of her husband's body and as the Queen of the Underworld. At the full moon, Isis is especially powerful in a maternal sense, so anything in your life that needs to be nurtured or protected, or any creative or fertility magic will respond to her help. The following invocation will call on her presence:

Isis, Great Mother, Queen,
Lady of Nature and Keeper of the Stars,
support and sustain me,
uplift and enfold me, enclosing me with your wings.
Bring me your bounty of riches and growth,
let me want for nothing that I truly need.
Heal me and guard me as I live my life.
May your loving presence be with me always,
Great Goddess whose heart beats at the centre of the world.

Roses are appropriate for Isis too. Burn white candles for her at the full moon. There is a lovely incense named for her that can be bought ready made from occult supply outlets, and that contains, among other ingredients, myrrh and rose petals.

DEMETER

Although Demeter is known chiefly as a Greek goddess, her roots are in pre-Hellenic times when she was a deity of fertility and growth. She is the Corn Mother, the one who brings the grain to ripeness, and the fertility of the earth depends on her care. Most people are familiar with the story of Demeter and Persephone, and many branches of the Craft celebrate their myth within ritual, as indeed it was celebrated at Eleusis for many, many hundreds of years.

In the story, Persephone was out on the hillside picking spring flowers when Hades saw her and abducted her, taking her into his subterranean domain. She wanted to return to the upper world, but Hades tricked her into eating some pomegranate seeds. Thus she was forced to spend part of the year in the Underworld but was allowed to return to daylight for the remaining months, so delineating the seasons. Part of the myth tells how Demeter set out in mourning to search for her daughter and in doing so neglected to tend to the crops, and so winter came to the land. During her search she performed a role almost identical to that of Isis, in which she became nurse to a human child whom she attempted to transform to immortality in the nightly fire. At the release of Persephone into the world, spring returns, and with her departure to the Underworld with the harvest, winter descends once more.

The legend of Demeter and Persephone is a purely female version of the Goddess and her dying and resurrecting lover/son, and as such is valuable to pagans who follow only the Goddess in their spiritual practice.

The following invocation to Demeter can be used to appeal to her for help with prosperity, fertility, and growth of all kinds. She is also of great comfort to anyone who has lost someone dear to her, or perhaps is grieving when a daughter leaves home to begin her own life:

> *Corn Mother, Lady of the Grain, who brings the harvest to birth,*
>> *bring me fertility and abundance too.*
> *You who know loss, comfort me when I'm in pain,*
>> *lay your sun-warmed hands on my brow.*
> *Ripen the seeds I have sown,*
>> *that I might reap the harvest in due time.*

ANU

This Celtic goddess originates in Ireland, though Black Annis of Leicestershire may be associated with her. There seems to be some confusion among modern sources as to whether she is also Dana or Danu, the Mother of the Tuatha te Danaan of prehistoric Ireland.

There are two hills in County Kerry, Ireland, named the Paps of Anu after her breasts. She is a goddess of cattle, grain, flowers, fire, and fertility. As an earth goddess she brings abundance, and as a lunar goddess she brings birth. It is thought that she may have been taken over by Saint Anne when Christianity came to Europe, and there are many wells named for Saint Anne in Brittany, which is a Celtic country renowned for its ancient healing springs. Modern Wiccan myth suggests that Anu is a bringer of magic and abundance at the full moon, and this would seem to fit well with her characteristics.

LAKSHMI

The gods churned the ocean for a hundred years till it turned to milk, from which came Amrita, the elixir of immortality, but also the Fourteen Precious Things, among them Lakshmi, who emerged seated on a lotus. Lakshmi, golden-skinned consort of the god Vishnu, is the bringer of abundance, wealth, fortune, and fertility, and her lotus throne is a symbol for the ripe and fecund womb. However, the abundance offered by Lakshmi refers to spiritual as well as material wholeness, and the lesson she brings us is that we need to be emotionally whole and open before material wealth can not only enter our lives but also bring satisfaction. True wealth is the contentment that springs from friendship, love, and family, along with a rich inner spiritual life. Lakshmi holds a lotus flower in her fingers, emblem of spiritual purity, but golden coins pour from her hands as well, and so she shows the balance between religious and material life and how bringing those two factors into equilibrium can promote harmony and joy. Her sacred animal is the cow, and she is sometimes seen with elephants who spray her with water, a sign of abundance and fertility, but also of the waters of life. In India she is worshipped in household shrines, especially by the women, and particularly at full moon, though she is also honoured at Diwali, the Festival of Lights. People pray to her for family health and wealth, and business people ask her for success in financial deals.

The god most called on at the full moon is the ancient horned god of Europe, sometimes called Herne or Cernunnos, and he partners the goddess when she is seen as the Great Goddess, the Earth Mother, or simply the Lady. He is the Horned One, usually the stag god, Lord of the Greenwood or Forests. However, his counterparts have come down to us from extreme antiquity. Inanna of Sumeria was sometimes portrayed flanked by stags; there is a horned Lord of the Animals from early Indian times; the Moon Bull was his brother, as was the ram-headed god. Horns were originally a sign of divinity, and both sex deities wore them. An alternative to him, much loved by modern witches, is the Greek goat-footed god Pan.

Be careful when calling the God into the circle. Many goddesses have specific male partners, and it would be a mistake to pair them with the wrong ones, as the mixing of energies could be extremely discordant. Here are a few of the partners: Lakshmi and Vishnu; Isis and Osiris; Inanna and Damuzi; the Lady and the Lord.

SOME MAGIC APPROPRIATE FOR THE FULL MOON

- Anoint deep pink candles with rose perfumed oil and burn them to bring romance into your life.

- Burn pale pink candles to bring friendship and enjoyment.

- Tie three knots into a length of golden cord or ribbon. As you do, say this chant:

    I tie these knots by power of three,
    may prosperity come to me.
    With harm to none, so mote it be.

    (Three is a number of the Goddess, and so using it in magic can bring very powerful results. Wear the cord day and night knotted round your wrist till the new moon.)

- For money magic, prime green candles with patchouli oil, stroking from base to centre and tip to centre, concentrating on your goal all the while, making sure that you specify that no harm must come to anyone in the realisation of the spell. Avoid getting oil on the wick or it will sputter and spit when you light it, and may flare up. Burn the candle every night for two weeks, keeping track of how much to burn at a time. An alternative (which will bring quicker results rather than steady growth) is to use an orange candle and cinnamon oil to be burned for a week. A gold candle anointed with frankincense can be used for a specific sum of money (for example, when there is something particular you need), and this should be put somewhere safe, such as in a fireproof container or in the sink, and allowed to burn down in one session.

- Bake fresh basil leaves into a cheesy dough mixture cut into rounds (use a special cutter or the rim of a cup or glass). Eat them in circle for a prosperity spell that you literally make a part of yourself.

- To bring success (for example, in career), charge a small piece of citrine and carry it in a pouch or your pocket for a month. To prime the crystal, place it in a bowl of water while in the ritual circle. Hold up the bowl and visualise the power of the moon entering the water and being conducted from there into the stone. If you can see the lunar energy as streaming light, then so much the better. Take the crystal out of the water and cup it in your hands, concentrating hard on imagining yourself successful in the area you have chosen. Make sure to say that no harm will come to anyone, and that you don't want your success at someone else's expense. Even if you are tempted to risk the karmic gauntlet over this, selfish magic has a habit of rebounding back hard on its maker.

BASIC FULL MOON RITUAL PATTERN

Refer to the appendix for a circle casting formula.

- Place fully opened flowers on the altar, especially opulent ones like roses, lilies, or peonies.

- Burn pure white or cream candles—church candles are very suitable.

- Use incenses such as rose, sandalwood, coconut, lotus, Isis, or ready-bought full moon incense.

- If you drum to raise energy, it should be powerful and deep. You could also chant or sing in a controlled yet emotional way, giving way to wilder vocalisations as the energy builds. Dance in a circle or on the spot.

- Call on the Goddess as the Mother, or invoke one of the deities mentioned in this section—or any others you know to be suitable.

- Magic for the full moon should concentrate on already established spell work such as that begun at new moon, or should be for definite wishes such as prosperity or success in a particular field, rather than new goals that need time to grow.

- Drink red or white wine, or grape juice. Eat round mooncakes. An especially nice mooncake recipe is given below:

Mooncakes

2½ tablespoons margarine or butter
3 rounded tablespoons sugar
3 rounded tablespoons plain flour
3 rounded tablespoons rolled oats
½ teasoon vanilla
1 tablespoon double cream (heavy cream)

Preheat oven to gas mark 5/190°C/375°F. Mix the cream, margarine, and sugar together. Stir in the flour, then the oats. In a separate bowl, beat the vanilla into the double cream, then stir into the flour mixture. Roll out on a floured board and shape into two-inch rounds with the hands. Place on a lightly greased baking tray and bake in the centre of the oven for about twelve minutes or until lightly brown. Cool and dust with castor (superfine) sugar and a little cinnamon powder. This recipe makes about six two-inch round mooncakes.

OTHER FULL MOON WORK

Scrying

The intense, psychically charged energy of the full moon is perfect for scrying. If you are working with a group, pass round a bowl of water or another scrying tool and each have a go. Sit relaxed but alert and let your eyes defocus slightly as you gaze into the surface. Let thoughts, images, or symbols come and go, either in the scrying surface itself or in your mind's eye. See what comes into your mind and use your intuition to interpret what you see, or tell those with you so that you can work it out together. Attempting clairvoyance with others of like mind helps the skills to develop. Of course you can also scry on your own, but it would be best to make sure you can have peace and quiet. Sit in a candlelit space and gaze into a crystal ball, witches' mirror, or bowl of water. With the latter you might find it helps to place something shiny in the bottom, such as a silver coin. Write down your insights, as, even if you can't make complete sense of them now, eventually something will happen that will put it all into place. This happened to me when I began attuning to my crystal ball. I looked in it only briefly and saw (in my mind, not the ball itself) a scarab beetle burst out of the earth and fly up toward the sun. Some time later I read that scarabs actually do rest under the earth and emerge into the sunlight. At that point in my life the message was that I would emerge from the difficulties I was experiencing on my spiritual path, and things would become open and clear again. Scarabs are a well-known occult symbol.

Capturing the Moon in a Bowl

Stand or sit where moonlight can reach you on a clear full moon night. If you are inside, draw back the curtains or blinds. Fill a bowl with water and fetch a small mirror. Place the mirror in the path of a moonbeam and direct the moonlight via the mirror into the bowl (in just the same way that people direct rays of sunlight with glass when they want to start a fire). Be prepared for the experience to be very intense. When I have been part of a circle where this was done, I felt the power of the moon enter me in much the same way as when having the moon drawn down on me by a priest.

Empowering Magical Tools

Your magical equipment can be placed in moonlight either prior to or after consecration so that it becomes imbued with lunar energy. If you like, you can hold the tools up to the moon and feel yourself drawing the power of the Goddess into them—this works especially well with wands and athames, or with a chalice filled with water (the water can be stored after and used for future lunar rites). An invocation to a particular deity can be helpful if you want them to be especially involved with your spiritual practice.

Chakra Water

If you feel you have a weakness, blockage, or imbalance in a particular chakra, pour some spring or mineral water into a glass tumbler or bottle that is the colour of the chakra you wish to heal. Leave it near a window overnight when the moon is full. If you can place it where the moon's rays will actually reach it at some point during the night, then so much the better, but don't worry if this isn't feasible, as the power of the moon will infuse the water anyway. Just before you go to bed the next night, bathe the relevant chakra with some of the water, then sip a little, visualising the chakra's colour as you do so, seeing the water as being energised with the qualities of that particular colour. Do this for three nights. This exercise can be extremely balancing. However, don't use it to enhance the chakra in question if there is nothing wrong, or you may create just the sort of imbalance it is intended to heal. The chakra colours are:

Base chakra: red

Navel chakra: orange

Solar plexus chakra: yellow

Heart chakra: green

Throat chakra: turquoise blue

Third eye chakra: violet

Crown chakra: white

Follow the aforementioned instructions, and this really will work. The reason that it is best done at bedtime is that the lunar energy may make you a little disorientated if the water is applied during the day. You may also have an enhanced dream life with significant symbols emerging while you are following this treatment, so it would be worth leaving a pen and paper by the bed to jot down any details on waking.

The full moon period lasts from the day before to the day after the point of maximum strength. After that the power begins to slowly but surely ebb, the peak of excitement calms, and the perfect silver-white lunar disk is gradually eaten away by darkness so that its right-hand edge recedes and loses symmetry. Little by little the whole world moves toward a state of rest.

initiation

The full moon is traditionally the optimum time for Craft initiations to take place. Whether someone is going to do a self-initiation or have another person perform the act for them, it is best for a period of contemplation and preparation to take place beforehand, to ascertain whether this is really the right course of action for the person involved. By accepting initiation, the person is taking on the responsibility of serving the Goddess and God in whatever way is appropriate for her, whether that is teaching, healing, developing occult gifts, or simply walking her own path to enlightenment. For some people, being initiated is a happy, exciting event that makes them feel accepted by the deities or the tradition they are entering, but for others the inner changes experienced, either then or later, can be profound, intense, and long lasting. Following one's deepest inner feelings over this is the best course to take. Initiation is like marriage—it should only be undergone as the result an of unshakeable inner conviction, and though it can be exited if it no longer feels appropriate, profound inner personal changes will have taken place that will be permanent. Having said that, people do sometimes grow in a different spiritual direction as the years pass, so there is no religious oath that can or should hold a person if she feels the urge to move on—anyone

who says otherwise is misinformed or on a power trip. Yes, it's probably true that initiation leaves its mark and will do so through all sub-
sequent lives, but then that's the case for every relationship and significant event we live through; it doesn't mean the former initiate is
forced to be a witch for the rest of her existence if she would rather,
for example, be a Druid or a Hindu . . . or even have no religion at all.
Nonetheless, many of us have been witches in prior lives and are
happy to return to this path.

Initiation is the key that opens an internal door for the person who
undergoes it willingly and without fear. For those at the beginning of a
particular spiritual journey, that door will be the entrance to psychic
development and to learning centred round the tradition they are to be
involved with. Many people come to initiation with their occult eyes
already quite open, and to them the rite will be a deepening of commitment and learning, and dedication to helping others along the way.
In the beginning sentence of this paragraph I mentioned undergoing
initiation without fear. It is absolutely essential that all people contem-
plating being initiated should be sure of the people who will induct
them, or, in the case of self-initiation, should be clear about his motives
and commitment. Undergoing initiation when there are doubts or
when one is distrustful of others involved can have emotional and psychological repercussions that can be quite difficult to deal with.

The following are my own preparations for initiations, followed by
both an initiation rite for a solitary and one for entrance into a group
or coven or a magical partnership. Anyone who wants to use these
preparations is welcome.

PREPARATION FOR INITIATION

These preparation guidelines are appropriate for either type of initiation.

- If you want to use a Craft or magical name, this should have been
  chosen before the date of the initiation, and after careful thought.
  Watch out for signs coming to you via dreams or through seem-
  ingly random events that suggest a name to you. My original

craft name revealed itself to me when the leaves of a certain tree tangled in my hair when I was out walking. It could have been a random incident, but something in me "knew" it was a sign that the associated tree was linked with my name . . . it just felt right.

- If this is to be initiation into a group or coven, then the candidate should have discussed everything thoroughly beforehand with all involved, so that she understands what is expected of her and what initiation can and can't do for her. Many groups require a waiting period of a year and a day before the rite can take place, and during this time the potential initiate should be learning all she can about the Craft. For those of us who have much prior knowledge and experience and who have practised solitary or within another tradition, then the waiting period may be shorter and may be more a matter of getting to know the other people to see whether they can work with us harmoniously. People doing a self-initiation will have to decide for themselves when they feel ready.

- If at all possible, the initiate should fast for a few hours before the rite. Don't impose this if there is any condition such as diabetes or low blood sugar, which would cause problems, and don't continue if faintness, headache, or any other form of illness is felt, as this will totally spoil the occasion.

- The person or people responsible for the initiation rite (obviously you if it's to be a self-initiation) should clean the room where it is to take place, put flowers on the altar and around the room, and set everything else up in readiness. A fresh white candle is needed for the initiate to light afterward, symbolising his new life. Make sure there is some sort of celebratory feast for after the initiation. A lovely custom some groups follow is for everyone to give the initiate "birthday" presents at the end of the ritual to welcome him into his new life.

- The candidate should have a cleansing bath, during which she immerses the whole of herself, including her head, at some point. (If, like me, the candidate doesn't like putting her face under water, then the rest of the head should be ducked and the face washed separately.) It's a nice idea to put herbs or dried flowers such as rose petals into the water and add some sea salt as well. Light candles round the bathroom if you want. If you don't have a bath, then make up a mixture that includes herbs and sea salt for the person to dowse herself with just before stepping out of the shower. Time should be taken to relax, slow the whole pace down, and begin to enter a meditative frame of mind. The best ritual bath of all, of course, is taken in a natural pool, waterfall, stream, or the sea, though that is an option for only a lucky few.

- When dry, the ritual robe should be donned, unless the choice is to go skyclad.

- If this is a group event, then there needs to be a quiet and warm candlelit place for the initiate to wait while the circle is swept and incense and candles are lit; if this is a solitary rite, then the ritual room itself can be used. The initiate should spend a little time thinking about the step he is about to take. It is, in a sense, a death (to the old spiritual way of being) and a rebirth (into the group, tradition, or path to be followed now, and into the service of the Goddess and God), and meditating on this fact can be a good way of readying oneself for the approaching rite. This suggestion is not meant to be scary, but to prepare one for the seriousness of the step about to be taken. Never forget that it should be a joyous happening as well. Some traditions expect their potential candidates to meditate for an hour or more beforehand, but this can be too long, leading to apprehension, butterflies, or loss of concentration.

- It goes without saying that no initiation should involve pain, fear or distress. In my opinion this includes the practice of pricking the thumb so that the measure can be smeared with the initiate's blood, or even that of blindfolding. We no longer live in a tribal society where feats of courage and endurance are necessary for survival. Initiation is undertaken voluntarily now, and the rite itself should reflect that fact. The practice some traditional groups follow of keeping the candidate in the dark about what to expect is, in my opinion, irresponsible. You wouldn't undergo childbirth unprepared and ignorant, and prior knowledge in no way spoils the wonder of the event itself. Deliberately frightening people is contemptible and could lead to serious emotional repercussions when the initiate enters the circle open and vulnerable and in dread—a far cry from Perfect Love and Perfect Trust.

Initiation Into a Coven or Group

The circle should have been swept and the candles and incense lit, but the actual casting needs to be left till the initiate is inside the space. The initiate should be brought to the edge of the ritual area and whomever will be performing the actual rite should say:

> *The step you are about to take is a serious one, though filled with joy as well. Once undertaken it can never be reversed. If you feel that you are not yet ready, or that this is not right for you, then say so now. Nobody will hold it against you. Do you wish to be initiated?*

If the initiate wants to delay or cancel the rite, then she should be definite at this point. Otherwise the initiate should confirm that she wants to go through with the initiation.

The initiator now says:

> *Will you serve the Goddess and God in whatever way is right for you? And will you help and guide others who seek this path?*

When and if the candidate has replied in the affirmative, the initiator continues:

> *Of your own free will, you have chosen to step upon a path that is ancient and yet unfolds afresh for each of us. Close your eyes and let me guide you into the circle.*

This is not the full-scale binding and blindfolding that takes place at traditional Wiccan initiations. However, closing your eyes and relying on another person to direct your progress requires a certain amount of trust and is symbolic of the Perfect Love and Perfect Trust spoken of within the Craft.

The initiator now leads the initiate into the western quarter of the circle and says:

> Now I will help you to kneel. I want you to tuck your head down and put your arms around your head. By entering the circle you are entering the womb again from which you will be born into a new life. Wait silently while we prepare for your birth.

The initiate is helped to kneel, head down, then the circle is cast in the usual way. The person conducting the initiation now sits next to the initiate and says:

> You wait in the west, the place of death and rebirth, held in the womb of the Goddess. The womb is the watery container in which we all are cradled. It is cauldron and chalice and Grail within which feelings are enhanced and rational defence is stripped away. Have the courage to face your feelings here. [A pause of up to a minute (use your intuition here; a minute may not seem long, but if you are waiting with closed eyes, experiencing your innermost feelings, then it can seem an eternity), then the initiator continues]: Now I will help you to rise, but you must keep your eyes shut. The birth process has begun.

The initiate is now helped to his feet and guided to the northern quarter, where the initiator says:

> Here in the north, the midnight place of earth and deepest mystery, all things gain form. Take a moment to feel your new body.

After a minute, the initiate is led to the eastern quarter and the initiator says:

You are born in the east, the place of air, and here you first draw breath. Open your eyes and see the light of your new life. [Pause for the initiate to open his eyes and reorient. This is a profound moment for most people. To the onlookers, even though there is hopefully a sense of magic and mystery to the proceedings, there has been an awareness of familiar, mundane surroundings. However, to the person at the focus of the rite, who has had his eyes closed all the while, this really is an emergence from a state in which he has gone into his own depths.]

The initiator speaks again:

Now come with me to the southern quarter.

At the southern quarter the initiator continues:

Here in the south, fiery place of self-determination and will, I ask you, Are you ready to take on the responsibility of your new life in the Craft? If so, then answer, Yes.

When the initiate has answered, the initiator then says:

You have been reborn into the Craft [leads the initiate into the centre of the circle]. *Welcome* [Craft name if one has been chosen, otherwise usual name] *priest/ess of the Goddess and the God. Take this candle and light it in honour of your new status. Burn it again every night till it is gone, and as you do so contemplate the step you have taken. May wisdom and joy surround you now and always. Blessed be.*

The new priest/ess should be handed the fresh white candle and should light it from one of the altar candles then place it in a holder provided.

Now other coven members can hug and welcome their new brother or sister, and cakes and wine can be followed by a celebratory feast and gift giving.

If you have just performed an initiation on somebody, then she needs to be cosseted for a while till she has had time to process the event. Don't send the initiate home immediately, but let her talk about the experience if she wants to. Make it clear that you are available if any insights or questions come up. Phone her the next day just to touch base, and arrange to see her within a few days. Most people will be bubbling over with excitement and joy after initiation, but for some the rite throws up deep-seated issues that they may need help to process. It is unkind, negligent, and irresponsible to abandon a person to deal with this alone, especially as she probably will not be able to discuss her involvement with the Craft freely for fear of condemnation or ridicule from outsiders.

Self-Initiation

Follow the aforementioned guidelines prior to the group initiation. As there will be no one to give you gifts afterward, it's a nice thought to find something to give yourself to mark the event, perhaps a ring or pendant that you can wear from this point on. A pentagram pendant would be an obvious choice, but it could be an ankh, a Goddess or God image, a crescent moon, a spiral, a special crystal or stone, or another symbol that can be worn either all the time or during rituals. Put a fresh white unlit candle and a holder on the altar. Give yourself plenty of time to prepare.

When you have had your cleansing bath and are adorned in whatever garb you have chosen to wear, light candles (though not the fresh white one) and incense, cast your circle, and then curl into a comfortable position lying on your side, or on your stomach with your head tucked into your arms, and close your eyes. Now think for a while about the fact that you are about to be reborn into a deeper way of being. You will still be the same person, but you will have taken a step that will open up much more for you, both within your own psyche and within your quest for wisdom, knowledge, and understanding.

When you are ready, open your eyes, stretch, and get up, then kneel before your altar. Spread your arms wide and say:

Gentle Lady, Fierce Lord, I offer myself in service to you. From now on I will walk the path that leads to you. I know I will find you within my own heart. I (name or Craft name) am now your priest/ess. I commit myself to learning, and to healing others along the way. I will develop my skills in ways that will further your work, ever respectful of the world in which I live, and of the needs and rights of others. Blessed be.

Now walk to the eastern quarter and say:

I stand before you a priest/ess of the Goddess and God. May I speak their truth, but only to those who are ready to hear.

Go to the southern quarter and say:

I stand before you a priest/ess of the Goddess and God. May I work with inspiration and creativity.

Go to the western quarter and say:

I stand before you, a priest/ess of the Goddess and God. May I use compassion and intuition in all I do.

Go to the northern quarter and say:

I stand before you, a priest/ess of the Goddess and God. May I grow closer to the mystery that lies at the heart of earth. Let me be steady and strong, for though my arms reach to the stars, my feet are rooted in the soil of this world.

Then return to the altar, light the fresh white candle, and say:

I stand in the centre, the place of Spirit where all the elements meet and are joined. So too am I made whole and a part of the unity of existence.

Place the candle in a holder on the altar. Light it again every night, thinking on your new life and your commitment to the Craft when you do so.

Have your celebratory feast, then sit for a while to enjoy the peace and protection of the circle, and the realisation of your new status as a priestess or priest of the Craft.

Initiation is not an ending but a beginning. In the years ahead the initiate will probably grow and change, and may even go on to explore other faiths and spiritual ways. The ideals that seem so concrete and perfect now may also be adapted, or even left behind as others emerge. Existence is not static; everything is in a state of evolution, including our spirituality. As we gradually experience the different aspects of life, our ideas change and evolve too, and so the theories and symbols that once seemed to suggest absolute truths reveal themselves to have been ciphers, and others take their place or alter them. At times we may come back to concepts we thought we had abandoned and see them in a new light or with a wider visual perspective. The key initiation provides is meant to unlock the door that opens on our true nature, for to know ourselves is to understand all of existence.

the last quarter

Excitement and tension slowly ebb away and the moon fades visibly night by night. At last she pauses once more, her right half vanished into darkness as though cloven by a razor-sharp blade. The waning half moon can often be seen during daylight, and this seems mystical to us, almost surreal. She floats in the sky from dawn until quite late in the morning, fading to papery white as the sky brightens, drifting across the heavens as the day progresses. The sense of stillness at this moon's quarter is somehow more peaceful, more of a release into decline and resolution than a breath drawn in anticipation. It is a period of relaxation that is not yet tinged with tiredness or lethargy. Both people and animals appear to behave in a more sensible fashion; the wild exuberance of the moon's waxing and full phases has settled into more seemly activity, with life proceeding at a steady, sure pace. Even the ocean tides are tamer and flatter.

The balance is more apparent than at first quarter because energies are winding down instead of increasing. With the gradual darkening comes restfulness. We are more ready to accept what cannot be changed, preparing to relinquish whatever hasn't worked out. Yet there is still a sense of magic that can be channelled now, still enough lunar power to help our lives along. It is a time to seek equilibrium in our own lives, firmly but peacefully letting go of failed projects, while working to eliminate remaining obstacles to viable growth. We can become more integrated at this point by the act of removing the so-called deadwood, and this includes bad habits. We can also work on self-acceptance by allowing ourselves to have human failings that can be worked on, but which must also be lived with while we endeavour to bring the changes about. This type of magical self-examination is inward and deeply personal. Finally, we can work on eliminating any conflicts and negativity within relationships, again doing so only from our own side of things, without trying to coerce, manipulate, or change the other parties involved. Sometimes it is necessary to realise that certain aspects of a relationship or situation can't be changed and can only be accepted and lived with if we wish to retain the positive factors as part of our lives.

Two goddesses relevant for the last quarter moon are the Ancient Egyptian goddess Maat and the Greek goddess of justice, Themis.

MAAT

This Egyptian goddess was sometimes said to be the daughter of the sun god Ra. Her name means "truth," and she represents those qualities of harmony, balance, and justice that maintain the order of the universe and keep it functioning in a predictable fashion. Maat was thought to have been there at the very beginning of creation, rising out of the formless void, and was the basis upon which all the other Egyptian deities were built. She is the regulating force behind universal law, and holds a sceptre, symbol of power wielded justly, and an ankh, which is the emblem of eternal life. Maat was sometimes seen as bestowing the breath of life upon the pharaoh via her ankh, and this is a compelling allusion, as breath and the power of creation are indivisibly linked in many religions. Maat was sometimes considered to be the Queen of Heaven, across which she guided the course of the sun, and the Queen of the Underworld, where she was part of the trial each soul was expected to go through after physical death. She is often depicted with outstretched wings, like Isis, but she is more commonly seen holding a pair of scales and with an ostrich feather in her headdress, and this was the feather against which the hearts of the dead were weighed in her scales, to judge whether they were pure enough to pass into the afterlife. Because of this her energy is appropriate for the last quarter lunar phase, when the end of the cycle and the descent into darkness is approaching, and letting go of the old can be appropriate.

Invoke Maat when you need to determine which parts of your life are working out and should go with you into the fresh lunar cycle after the next new moon. Anything that doesn't match up should be gently and lovingly discarded. The same goes for relationships, when the factors that are causing disruption or pain need to be healed and integrated or let go of forever. Ask Maat to help you examine any issue that is causing you problems, so that you can decide the best course of action to resolve, release, or otherwise improve the problems.

RITE TO RESTORE BALANCE

This rite can be done with or without casting a circle.

On the day or night of the exact waning half moon, prepare a quiet space and light candles and a soothing incense such as sandalwood. Sit or stand relaxed but quite straight. Think very clearly about whatever it is you wish to sort out. This needs to be an issue over which you are finding it difficult to make a decision. Try to imagine what your life would be like according to which course of action is taken. Then call on Maat with words similar to the following:

> O Maat, ancient Universal Queen,
> Lady of heaven, earth, and the realms beyond death,
> I need your wise council to resolve my life.
> My heart is troubled and my mind knows no rest.
> I beg you to weigh my doubts in your scales.
> Help me decide, help me to choose.

Imagine that Maat is weighing your question, balancing each aspect of it against the feather of truth, so that you will know what to let go of and what to change, and last of all what to keep in its present form. Sometimes it helps to hold out both hands, palms up, and visualise the problem in one hand and the feather of Maat in the other, as though your hands are the scale pans; think along the lines of "If I do such and such, how will that be?" then wait to see if either hand feels heavier than the other; if the hand holding the suggested solution feels heavier, then it may not be the right one, but if it feels lighter, then this may be the answer you have been looking for. An alternative would be to imagine two different solutions, one in each hand, and see which one weighs less.

Then let go of the issue for a while. As the dark moon approaches, begin to look for signs or for vivid dreams, or just strong intuition that carries an answer for you. Trust that the answer will come.

THEMIS

Themis is a Greek goddess of justice, law, and order. She played a similar role to that of Maat in that she was responsible for judging the souls of the dead and thus deciding whether or not they would go into the Afterlife; it is almost certain that she has taken over certain qualities of Maat. She is the origin of justice as seen in statue form in front of courthouses, and also the Justice card of tarot. She usually holds scales in one hand and a sword in the other, and sometimes she is portrayed blindfolded to represent the unbiased and indiscriminate quality of true justice that cannot be swayed by appearances. Themis was the daughter of the earth goddess Gaia, and this suggests that she had her origins in a much older culture than the Hellenic. It is sometimes thought that she was the original presiding deity at the Delphic oracle, before the *pythia* or oracular priestesses of the Goddess were displaced by patriarchal Apollo, and this may be why she was thought to be the mother of the three Fates; it would also explain why she was often seated on a tripod stool, just as the oracular priestesses were.

Themis may be appealed to in place of Maat, and she fulfils a similar function.

WORKING WITH THE LAST QUARTER ENERGIES

This is a time for peaceful rest and contemplation, the point of balance when it is possible to review magical work and gain some insights into what needs to be eliminated as the moon moves toward dark. Although it is possible to begin banishing work from about three days after the full moon, in some ways it is often better to wait till the energies are really ebbing. The last quarter is the ideal time to assess what needs to be relinquished or banished and what needs to be balanced, integrated, or otherwise healed.

This is also the best of times to think through any sort of diet or health regime so that it can be embarked upon over the remaining days of the waning moon. Improving one's health usually entails eliminating bad eating habits or the buildup of toxins in the system, or getting harmful habits under control. The reason why this type of planning responds so well to thinking through at last quarter is because it is a moment of balance when extremes are not so evident, and so working out a sensible routine is easier than at other times. Many a self-improvement plan has failed because of a lack of moderation; it is ulti-mately easier to stick to something if it incorporates temperance rather than going to enthusiastic but militant extremes.

Sorting through relationship problems is more likely to be done with equanimity now, as well. It can be productive to sit down with a partner and allow the peace and calm to come into consciousness so that both parties are less defensive than would often be the case. If you are experiencing conflict with a loved one, sometimes it works just to hold hands and say nothing for a while, but breathe deeply in unison so that your vibrations synchronise. Out of this equilibrium, you may find that one or both of you begin to spontaneously and tranquilly voice your concerns. If this happens, let the issues surface and then begin to talk about suggestions as to how you can fix the problems. Hopefully you will be able to at least begin to see a way to mend the damaged areas of your relationship.

The moon's quarters are worth working with if only in meditation, when they provide a restful stopping point in the monthly cycle of waxing and waning activity. Once the moment of last quarter has passed, energies grow flatter and flatter as the moon wanes.

the indian lunar zodiac

Everybody has heard of the solar zodiac, which is the belt of constellations through which the sun appears to pass on its route through the
seasons. But there is another zodiac that is not so familiar, the Indian
lunar zodiac, based, as the title suggests, on the path of the moon rather
than that of the sun through the fixed stars. Indeed, in Indian astrology,
the moon is of greater importance than the sun in horoscope interpretation. Discovering that there is a form of astrology based on the
moon's journey is very exciting for pagans since it brings the Goddess
back to this ancient art/science and provides a balance for the concept
of putting the male/solar principle at the heart of the birth chart. In
medieval times in Europe the lunar zodiac was almost certainly in use,
but it has vanished from Western astrology since the Renaissance, having been regarded with suspicion by the Church, who, quite rightly,
associated the moon with magic. So we have lost our Western lunar
zodiac, to our great detriment—though other cultures, including the
Arabic, have used a similar astrological model, and Chinese astrology
still employs an approach based on an original lunar zodiac, though the
part the moon once played in this has fallen out of use.

The Hindu system of lunar mansions, or *Nakshatras,* as they are
called, is much older than the solar zodiac. In India it is used alongside

of and interwoven with the sun-based system, and predictive astrology, character analysis, and synastry (the astrology of relationships) depend on it. Vedic or Hindu astrology is a vast and complex subject that deserves study in its own right, and it is impossible to more than skim the surface of it here, but nonetheless it is worth taking a look at the Nakshatras and seeing briefly how they affect the birth chart.

There are twenty-seven Nakshatras, or lunar mansions, since the moon takes just over twenty-seven days to traverse the whole 360 degrees of the zodiac. Each Nakshatras is 13 degrees 20 minutes long, this being the approximate distance the moon travels in twenty-four hours. The moon is said to be a god who visits one of his twenty-seven wives (the Nakshatras) each night in succession during his journey through the month. The first Nakshatra, Aswini, begins with 0 degrees Aries; the second, Bharani, with 13 degrees 20 minutes Aries; and so on round the complete zodiacal circle. Every Nakshatra has a ruling planet, and these include the moon's nodes Rahu and Ketu, and each has a ruling deity. Each also rules a part of the body and has an associated animal and related qualities. Each planet in a birth chart will fall within one of the Nakshatras, the most important of these being the moon. The Indian lunar zodiac provides additional factors that influence our lives on earth according to the way they are reflected in our horoscopes.

Before describing the Nakshatras and their attributes, it is necessary to explain the difference between Western and Indian astrology generally. Western astrology is based on the tropical zodiac that begins with the Spring or Vernal Equinox and 0 degrees Aries, the point at which the sun originally crossed the ecliptic at this time of year. At one time the actual constellation of Aries lined up exactly with the symbolic zodiac sign, but this is no longer the case because of the precession of the equinoxes wherein a wobble in the earth's rotational axis causes the signs to apparently move backward by one degree every seventy-two years. Consequently, the actual equinoctial point is no longer in Aries. Vedic astrology, however, uses the sidereal zodiac, which is tied to the fixed stars rather than the ecliptic (the sun's apparent path) and, therefore, does not change. Although the two systems seem contradictory, in fact both are valid. Western astrology works still, despite being based on a symbolic rather than an actual starting point, because so much of the way we live and understand our spirituality is through symbols that point to rather than define inner truth. Hindu astrology works on a different level, is much more concerned with events, partnership compatibility, and so on, and describes a different but complementary aspect of our astrological makeup. The two zodiacs, Eastern and Western, are now between twenty-three and twenty-four degrees apart, so if you know the degree of your moon and other planets in the signs, then you need to subtract about twenty-three degrees from each to convert them to the sidereal positions, remembering that there are thirty degrees in a zodiacal sign. This means that for many people most of their horoscope is placed in earlier astrological signs, and only people with placements toward the end of signs will keep the same designations, though the planetary degrees will have changed. So, for example, if you have moon in the first roughly two-thirds of Taurus in the Western system, you will find that it is in Aries in the Eastern system.

The following is a description of the twenty-seven Nakshatras, which will give their colouration to any planet situated in them, but especially to the moon in a horoscope (don't forget that the zodiac signs given are according to the sidereal rather than the tropical zodiac).

1 Aswini: 0 degrees 13 minutes Aries to 20 degrees 00 minutes Aries

Ruling planet: Ketu

Ruling deity: the Aswini Kumars, the twin sons of the sun,
    who are physicians/healers

Body area: upper foot

Creature: horse

Aswini, which is symbolised by a horse or horse and rider, represents beginnings, as one might expect from its placement at the start of

Aries. People with this Nakshatra prominent in their birth charts have qualities of swiftness, decisiveness, healing, and courage, though its more negative side shows in rashness or quick-tempered behaviour. They may be athletic, quick-witted, and could become doctors, sports people, or involved with the equestrian world. These people will probably be well dressed.

2 Bharani: 13 degrees 20 minutes Aries
    to 26 degrees 40 minutes Aries

Ruling planet: Venus

Ruling deity: Yama, the god of death

Body area: lower foot

Creature: elephant

The symbol for Bharani is the yoni, the triangle of the female sex organs. This makes sense when paired with the deity presiding over death, for out of fatality and struggle, out of endings and relinquishment, come new growth and rebirth (just as a child is born from the unsettling contractions of the womb). This is seen in Western paganism in the wide open vulva of the Sheelah Na Gig, the Crone who represents the death all must face in order for regeneration to take place, for we cannot have unchecked growth. The other interesting link here is between the ruling planet and deity, for Venus is concerned with sexual matters, and sex is not only called the little death because of the total giving up of self that is required, but because sex and death are intimately linked in the cycle of regeneration. People born under Bharani can be ardent and passionate, especially where love affairs are concerned, but they are also incredibly loyal to those they care about. They are idealistic and cheerful, but they often need to learn more patience. Their lives may be filled with struggles and endings out of which much growth, both emotional and spiritual, can arise. Bharani people can be athletic and active. They are very creative and so often follow careers in the arts, though they are good with children and child-related professions too.

3 Krittika: 26 degrees 40 minutes Aries
   to 10 degrees 00 minutes Taurus

Ruling planet: sun

Ruling deity: Agni, the fire god

Body area: head

Creature: goat

Like their symbol, the axe or blade, Krittika people can be sharp and cutting. They are very proud and have a fiery nature that can get them into trouble by causing conflict in their interchanges with others. They often have a voracious appetite for many areas of life, and this includes food and sex. However, they can be practical too, and are not afraid to face difficulties, which they tackle with determination. When behaving negatively, Krittika people can become exhausted through overdoing, or can act too hastily to take care of the details. They make good crafts-people, especially in trades that use fire, such as smithing. They are often very ambitious, and consequently may become wealthy through their own efforts.

4 Rohini: 10 degrees 23 minutes Taurus
   to 20 degrees 00 minutes Taurus

Ruling planet: moon

Ruling deity: Brahma, the creator god

Body area: brow

Creature: snake

One myth associated with Rohini is that she was the moon's favourite wife because of her sensuality and beauty, and those born with this Nakshatra emphasised are often very alluring too. The sign for Rohini is a cart, the kind that is drawn by slow-moving beasts such as oxen, and Rohini people are very pleasant and steady, earthy and easy-going, though they can be critical at times. Their way of dealing with obstacles to their goals is to keep doggedly going, simply sidestepping anything that blocks their progress. They are often drawn to occupations involving agriculture, or the arts, fashion, or beauty therapy. They have a tendency to become too involved in the material world and need to look beyond to life's deeper meaning.

5 Mrigashira: 23 degrees 20 minutes Taurus
   to 6 degrees 40 minutes Gemini

Ruling planet: Mars

Ruling deity: Chandra, or the moon

Body part: eyebrows

Creature: snake

Because their symbol is the deer, Mrigashira people are often quick-moving, nervous, and always on the go. They are witty and talkative, and often have a flair for languages, but, like their ruling deity the moon, they can be subject to shifting moods, inconstancy, and changing affections. They may be fond of travelling, which reflects their deep-seated restlessness and dissatisfaction with life. Many Mrigashira people do well in careers that involve buying and selling or working in the media.

6 Ardra: 6 degrees 40 minutes Gemini
   to 20 degrees 00 minutes Gemini

Ruling planet: Rahu

Ruling deity: Rudra, god of storms; he is sometimes seen as
   the Lord of Wild Creatures, giving him something of the
   essence of the Horned God

Body part: eyes

Creature: dog

The connection between the ruling deity of Ardra, Rudra god of storms and destruction, and its symbol, the teardrop, is obvious. Ardra folk may go through some upheavals and endings in life, but from this comes fresh growth and a more satisfactory way of being. The teardrop turns to a sparkling jewel when sunlight strikes it. Rudra's storms can remove the obstacles that were blocking the way to a better life. Ardra people need to be careful of hasty or sarcastic speech that can wound others and bring about the very conflicts that cause them problems. These people can be both deeply emotional and also motivated to explore life on a more profound level than is common, and so they can come to a better understanding of the spiritual basis of existence and of nature and the world we inhabit. Because of the loss and sorrow sometimes experienced in their own lives, people born under Ardra can often make very good social workers or counsellors, or work in any other occupation where it is an advantage to be able to understand what other people are going through. More than any others, they know that there is always sunshine after rain, and that both are necessary for growth and flowering to take place.

7 Punavarsu: 20 degrees 00 minutes Gemini
   to 3 degrees 20 minutes Cancer

Ruling planet: Jupiter

Ruling deity: Aditi, goddess of infinity, wide open spaces,
   and unboundedness, both physically and spiritually

Body part: nose

Creature: cat

Punavarsu is represented by a quiver full of arrows, or sometimes by a single arrow, and this is shown in its natives desire to shoot toward distant spiritual goals—very much in keeping with the qualities of their ruling planet, Jupiter. They are adaptable people who are often philosophical or religious, their ideas unbounded by practical concerns, and they are often content with very little. However, they are extremely generous and may have many friends, as others are attracted to their compassionate natures. Sometimes Punavarsu-influenced people can appear detached because of their unworldly leanings, and indeed they can exhibit hermitlike tendencies despite their popularity. They are imaginative and can make talented writers, poets, and teachers.

8 Pushya: 3 degrees 20 minutes Cancer
to 16 degrees 20 minutes Cancer

Ruling planet: Saturn

Ruling deity: Brihaspati, the god of magic and prayer, whose chanting
helped to create the universe

Body part: face

Creature: goat

Pushya people are often spiritual in a religious or devotional way, and
may spend much of their lives searching for life's deepest meanings.
They are also compassionate and may wish to nurture others, especially
in any way that will bring them to spiritual understanding. All this is
reflected by their symbol, which is the wheel, the circle, or a flower, all
icons connected with or suggestive of spirituality or spiritual growth.
They may be overemotional at times, and when feeling negative they
can take unintentional slights to heart. Those with this Nakshatra
emphasised in their birth charts are usually very honest and ethical.
They may be attracted to the priesthood or to some other area of life
where wisdom and a love of truth are essential.

9 Aslesha: 16 degrees 40 minutes Cancer to 00 degrees Leo

Ruling planet: Mercury

Ruling deity: Sarpas, the serpent god

Body part: ears

Creature: cat

The sign for Aslesha is the serpent, especially a coiled serpent, and in
keeping with the occult symbolism of this creature, people influenced
by Aslesha may be extremely gifted in an occult sense. They can also
be skilled with words and very persuasive. The more negative mani-
festations of this Nakshatra can lead to underhand behaviour, devious-
ness, or sarcasm. Used positively, the energies of Aslesha can lead to
great spirituality, though care must be taken that its influence doesn't

manifest in depression, rebelliousness, or impracticality. Because they are multigifted and capable, Aslesha people can put their talents to use in many different fields and are often quite wealthy.

10 Magha: 00 degrees Leo to 13 degrees 20 minutes Leo

Ruling planet: Ketu

Ruling deity: the Pitris, who are one's ancestors in direct family line, but who can be seen, in a wider sense, as inner plane guides or spiritual beings overseeing our development (whether you understand these as actual entities or as a wiser part of your own psyche)

Body part: chin/lips

Creature: rat

This Nakshatra falls in Leo, and its natives can display many of the qualities normally associated with Leo, both good and bad; these include ambition, arrogance, creativity, benevolence, generosity, and overbearing behaviour. These qualities tie in nicely with the symbol for Magha, which is the throne or throne room. There is something very regal about Magha people, and they often make good lawyers, judges, and business people.

11 Purva Phalguni: 13 degrees 20 minutes Leo
    to 26 degrees 40 minutes Leo

Ruling planet: Venus

Ruling deity: Bhaga, a god of fortune

Body part: right hand

Creature: rat

The symbol for this Nakshatra is a bed or reclining couch, and this is apt, as people born under its aegis are often very fortunate and able to enjoy the good things of life without putting too much effort into earning them. Having said that, they are vital, active people who may seek the limelight and become despondent if it doesn't shine on them; they may suffer from depression-induced inertia. They can be the soul of generosity. Purva Phalguni-influenced individuals may find careers in the performing arts or other areas that bring them fame or recognition.

12 Uttara Phalguni: 26 degrees 40 minutes Leo
to 10 degrees 00 minutes Virgo

Ruling planet: the sun

Ruling deity: Aryaman, another god of luck and fortune

Body part: left hand

Creature: cow

Individuals influenced by Uttara Phalguni are popular, likeable, and hard working, though they are also fortunate and gain recognition and monetary rewards for their hard work. At their worst they can be vain social climbers who think the world owes them a living, but usually they are generous natured and ready to help those less fortunate than themselves. The symbolism of a bed, couch, or other place where one might relax is carried over into this Nakshatra, and many of the qualities are the same as in Purva Phalguni, though individuals influenced by the current lunar mansion are more willing to work for what they have. They can often be found in managerial positions, or other occupations that put them in authority or in the public eye, such as the media.

13 Hasta: 10 degrees 00 minutes Virgo
to 23 degrees 20 minutes Virgo

Ruling planet: the moon

Ruling deity: Savitri, the sun god, but sometimes seen as a goddess
who is the daughter of the sun

Body part: fingers

Creature: buffalo

As their symbol of the hand implies, those born under Hasta are often very clever and dexterous, quite inventive, in fact, and can turn their hands to a number of different skills; they are often artistic or have abilities in the field of handicrafts. They are busy individuals who nonetheless can radiate calm and serenity, though the calmness is based more on detachment than personal integration and balance. They are good communicators, but this very mental agility can sometimes lead them into the wrong company or occupations because they tend to analyse rather than trust their instincts and therefore can fall prey to persuasive talk—which may be why they are traditionally accused of being prone to treachery, thievery, and other unsavoury characteristics. Because of this weakness, they need to become more emotionally orientated and empathetic. However, they are hard workers who excel as teachers, artists, and craftspeople.

14 Chitra: 23 degrees 20 minutes Virgo
to 6 degrees 40 minutes Libra

Ruling planet: Mars

Ruling deity: Tvashtri, an artisan deity whose craftwork is the fashioning of the worlds

Body part: neck

Creature: tiger

Like their symbol, the lustrous and mysterious pearl, Chitra-born people are alluring and beautiful and will often be expensively and attractively dressed, even if their income is limited. They are artistic, articulate, and often well read, educated, or academically gifted as well. Although they can be quite charming and diplomatic, their negative side can manifest as wilfulness and the refusal to back down in an argument or when they want their own way, as can be surmised from their Mars rulership. Having said that, people influenced by Chitra are generally philosophical, fair minded, and diplomatic, though they can be critical. They do well in occupations involving the arts, jewellery, alternative healing, and business.

15 Swati: 6 degrees 40 minutes Libra to 20 degrees 00 minutes Libra

Ruling planet: Rahu

Ruling deity: Vayu, the god of wind, sometimes the wind itself

Body part: chest

Creature: buffalo

The symbol for Swati is the shoot of a plant, fresh and tender but growing determinedly toward the light. Swati people are often diplomatic and friendly, but can appear fairly quiet and unassuming. Despite this, they are fiercely independent and hate to be tied down in any way. However, a certain seeking of knowledge and a desire to be on the move, either literally or intellectually, illustrates the restlessness of their airy ruling deity. Even so, those with the Nakshatra of Swati emphasised in their chart can be very well-balanced and integrated individuals once they determine a direction in life. The plant symbolism can be seen in the spiritual growth they are able to make, though sometimes they may be drawn to materialism. They are capable of being deeply religious or extremely learned in an academic sense, and they are often artistic or musical. They do well in professions that exercise their capacity for learning and their hunger for knowledge.

16 Vishaka: 20 degrees 00 minutes Libra
   to 3 degrees 20 minutes Scorpio

Ruling planet: Jupiter

Ruling deity: Indra, the supreme god, and Agni, the god of fire

Body part: breast

Creature: tiger

The symbol for this Nakshatra is the triumphal arch, and those who have a strong Vishaka influence are proficient at getting what they want from life. They are clever and persuasive, and extremely charismatic. Vishaka people can be torn between their lower and higher natures, wanting to aspire spiritually but sometimes being pulled by the temptation to overindulge in food, sex, or other delights of the flesh. There is nothing wrong with enjoying the pleasures of the world, as long as they are kept in balance with other aspects of life, and Vishaka teaches the extremes, which drive the soul to find that balance if it is ever to know peace. Although they can exhibit extreme courage, they can also be ambitious and ruthless if they forget to see the rights and outlook of others. They excel in careers like politics or corporate business, where willpower and strategical thinking are required.

17 Anuradha: 3 degrees 20 minutes Scorpio
   to 16 degrees 40 minutes Scorpio

Ruling planet: Saturn

Ruling deity: Mitra, a deity associated with amicable relationships

Body part: stomach

Creature: deer

Like their symbol the lotus, an emblem for spiritual growth, Anuradha people are spiritual seekers wishing to attain some form of wisdom or enlightenment. In keeping with their ruling deity, they cultivate friendship and wish to preserve equilibrium between themselves and others, and are good at seeing everyone's point of view. They can, however, be quite ambitious and are usually successful in whatever career they put their energies into.

18 Jyeshta: 16 degrees 40 minutes Scorpio to 00 degrees Sagittarius

Ruling planet: Mercury

Ruling deity: Indra, the ruling deity

Body part: right side

Creature: deer

Under Jyeshta, people are intense, determined, but generous and supportive to those they love, though they need to beware of allowing themselves to be manipulative to get what they want. The symbolic icon for this Nakshatra is a fringed umbrella or dangly earring, both indications of status in Indian society. The choice for Jyeshta is between worldly rank and spiritual growth, though people under its influence may be tempted to seek religious or spiritual recognition for the standing it confers in the eyes of the community. Nonetheless, they usually want to rise by their own efforts, and excel in careers where hard work brings them gradually into the public eye, and where they are known to be self-made.

19 Mula: 00 degrees Sagittarius to 13 degrees 20 minutes Sagittarius

Ruling planet: Ketu

Ruling deity: Nirriti, goddess of bad luck or destruction

Body part: left side

Creature: dog

The symbol for Mula is either a bunch of roots and stems tied firmly, or the tail of a lion crouched to spring—both of these are similar pictorially. Despite the qualities of its ruling deity, the Nakshatra of Mula often produces people who are very fortunate or successful. However, they may find that their material acquisitions or conquests don't bring them the satisfaction they would wish, and that only striving after spirituality will really fulfil them. It is when they put all their efforts into self-aggrandisement that these people feel the backlash from the ruling deity, Nirriti, who lays waste to their aspirations. Mula natives are clever, well read, and have penetrating insight. They can do well in the political arena or the field of law.

20 Purva Ashadha: 13 degrees 20 minutes Sagittarius
   to 26 degrees 40 minutes Sagittarius

Ruling planet: Venus

Ruling deity: Apah, the god of the waters

Body part: back

Creature: monkey

The symbol for this Nakshatra is the elephant's tusk, and just as the elephant is reputed to be wise, so can people born under Purva Ashadha be possessed of great wisdom. Their philosophical and enduring nature helps them to ride out life's ups and downs. Like water that gradually wears down obstacles, they endure to the end if they want something badly enough. They have expansive personalities, in keeping with the position of this lunar mansion enclosed by Sagittarius, and when they are behaving negatively they can be quite loud and raucous. Their major quest in life is very often a spiritual one, and they can be inspired writers or teachers who pass this knowledge on to others. However, Purva Ashadha people must be careful not to settle for less than they are worth in the mistaken belief that a spiritual path means a path of self-denial.

21 Uttara Ashadha: 26 degrees 40 minutes Sagittarius
   to 10 degrees 00 minutes Capricorn

Ruling planet: the sun

Ruling deity: Vishva, a blending of many god forms and their attributes

Body part: waist

Creature: mongoose

These people are often very well liked. They are witty, funny, and vivacious, and yet can pursue study and the acquisition of knowledge ardently. Like their ruling deity (or rather, collection of deities), they epitomise the essence of spirituality, and they can be extremely serious in their search for knowledge and meaning, sometimes to the extent of living in a fairly austere fashion. They, like Purva Ashadha, have the elephant's tusk as their emblem, and this sign connects these two Nakshatras with the elephant-headed god Ganesha, who has a sense of fun and lightheartedness despite being wise and compassionate. Just as Ganesha can remove obstacles from one's path, so can people born under this Nakshatra triumph over the pitfalls of any enterprise they espouse. They are great readers. They also enjoy travelling, which sometimes attracts them to a career in the armed forces. They may have equestrian links as well.

22 Sravana: 10 degrees 00 minutes Capricorn
to 23 degrees 20 minutes Capricorn

Ruling planet: the moon

Ruling deity: Vishnu, the preserver

Body part: genitals

Creature: monkey

Sravana people are usually extremely ethical. They can be fascinated by ancient history, and especially very old forms of religion or spirituality, and have a spiritual bias as well as a tendency to be humanitarian. They have a talent for languages and for passing on knowledge verbally, which can make them excellent teachers, lecturers, public speakers, or journalists. The flip side of this can result in sharp-tongued interchange or idle gossip if their need to express themselves verbally is repressed.

23 Dhanistha: 23 degrees 20 minutes Capricorn
to 6 degrees 40 minutes Aquarius

Ruling planet: Mars

Ruling deity: the Vasus, gods of material wealth and beneficence

Body part: anus

Creature: lion

The symbol for Dhanistha is a drum, and people with this Nakshatra prominent in their charts often have a good sense of rhythm both for music and for dance. But the drumbeat is also a metaphor for the heartbeat of the universe, and Dhanistha-influenced people may be stirred to awaken to a knowledge of the energies that lie within and behind the world of form. In their personal lives, they can be either very giving, understanding, and humanitarian, or else contentious, thriving on conflict. For them, overcoming aggression and discord is vital if they are to experience happiness. Musicians and doctors are often found in this Nakshatra.

24 Shatabisha: 6 degrees 40 minutes Aquarius
   to 20 degrees 00 minutes Aquarius

Ruling planet: Rahu

Ruling deity: Varuna, cosmic god of the sea

Body part: right thigh

Creature: horse

The sign for this Nakshatra is the circle, a symbol of infinity and spiritual truth, and Shatabisha people are often concerned with philosophical and esoteric learning. They can make gifted astrologers. But in mundane terms a circle circumscribes, it makes a boundary between inside and outside, and this is sometimes indicative of the self-contained nature of Shatabisha individuals, who can allow their self-imposed solitude to turn into isolation. They need to reach out from their reclusive lives and connect with and nurture others if they are to realise their own power and wisdom.

25 Purva Bhadra: 20 degrees 00 minutes Aquarius
   to 3 degrees 20 minutes Pisces

Ruling planet: Jupiter

Ruling deity: Ajaikapada, an obscure deity sometimes
   called the one-footed goat god

Body part: left thigh

Creature: lion

These people can be great worriers and are nervous and highly strung. However, they have a profound and deep grasp of life and death. The emblem for this Nakshatra is the platform on which a corpse is laid when awaiting the funeral, and is symbolic of its natives' capacity to stand at the gateway between the worlds that swings wide for us all at birth and death, and to grasp the meanings of existence. Purva Bhadra people can be fiery, passionate, and articulate, and yet they often have a hidden side and hold back those traits they would not wish others to see. When they are angered they can be harsh and hurtful. Yet at the heart of their disruptive behaviour is the drive for the transformation and self-realisation that can lead to spiritual wholeness—though the negative manifestation of this can be a morbid preoccupation with death. They can become morticians or, equally, psychologists, both occupations involved with the hidden realms of being. Another occupation that would suit them would be nursing the terminally ill, maybe in a hospice, and this nurturing others into the planes beyond the material level of being can bring great peace and understanding to Purva Bhadra natives.

26 Uttara Bhadra: 3 degrees 20 minutes Pisces
   to 16 degrees 40 minutes Pisces

Ruling planet: Saturn

Ruling deity: Ahirbudhnya, the serpent deity concerned
   with Kundalini energy

Body part: shins

Creature: cow

These people can be ethical, frugal, and humanitarian. Their sign also is connected with the funeral bed or platform, and they, like the previous Nakshatra's natives, can have a profound understanding of the meaning of death, though in the case of Uttara Bhadra this understanding goes further, encompassing regeneration, as shown by the serpent that, as Kundalini energy, facilitates our spiritual development and eventual enlightenment. Although capable of passion and emotional fire, Uttara Bhadra people are more balanced and less prone to anger than those of Purva Bhadra. They are skilled and deep thinkers, with an astute understanding of human nature, and have a love for their fellow humans though, even so, they may act like hermits at times. Those who live a life of retreat or contemplation, including monastic or other religious withdrawal, often have strong Uttara Bhadra placements.

27 Revati: 16 degrees 40 minutes Pisces
  to 30 degrees 00 minutes Pisces

Ruling planet: Mercury

Ruling deity: Pushan, god of possessions and guardian of travellers

Body part: ankles

Creature: elephant

Revati people are sympathetic and caring, and make good counsellors or social workers, but they need to be careful not to take too much on board from other people, since they are very receptive and find it hard to refuse to help. The sign for Revati, like that of Dhanistha, is a drum, but in this case it is the type of drum used solely for marking time or pace, and this Nakshatra is concerned with the rhythm of life as marked out by the seasons and the measurement of days and years as delineated by the course of solar and lunar journeying. So Revati natives have an understanding of nature and the joy to be found in living in accord with natural cycles and, consequently, can be attracted to country living.

As stated previously, the moon is the most important planet to consider when looking up your placements in the Nakshatras. The ascendant comes next, followed by the sun and the other planets. The Indian lunar zodiac is extremely old, as are lunar zodiacs in general, though it is not as ancient as some current writers claim. In the West, with our emphasis on individualism, we place the sun at the centre of the chart and give it the greatest importance. In India, where the family and community take precedence over the needs of the individual, the moon, which stands for all that is caring, traditional, and nurturing, is deemed to be of greater relevance. Perhaps we need to study both systems and bring them into balance. As Westerners we would find it difficult to live as Hindu people do, and would find the close but extended family circle restrictive; but we have lost much of value, such as support, caring, and unquestioning loyalty, which only a familylike setup can provide. Perhaps studying the lunar zodiac, along with becoming open to the moon's gifts of caring and nurturing, could teach us the qualities we need to restore to our relationships if we are to enjoy a healthier and more harmonious society.

old moon

Gradually, gently, quietly, the power of the moon winds down, till the frenetic activity of full moon seems a distant memory. Both animals and people go about their business more slowly and with less vigour. Everything seems to turn increasingly inward, and there is little energy available for anything new. The lunar orb fades to an increasingly narrow crescent and its right face is dark. This is a peaceful time with the same slight melancholy that comes to us with autumn and the decreasing of the year's vitality. It is unwise to start fresh projects now, but instead work should be done on eliminating deadwood from our lives, banishing the unwanted and clearing the ground before the new moon arrives. Nights are darker, but the approach to dawn reveals the shrinking curve of silver-white, which is the emblem of the Wise Grandmother or Crone. Toward the end of this phase, lethargy or tiredness increases and enthusiasm is very low. It often takes longer to accomplish tasks, and transactions and negotiations are plagued with delays and misunderstandings—not always, but often enough for a pattern to be seen.

At last the moon's light is swallowed by blackness, and we are left with a fathomless and profound inner dark in which the potential for future growth is stored. Like the debris of many seasons' leaves and loam, our hidden selves contain a rich and potent store of discarded or repressed experiences that can reveal valuable material that can be transformed to our own benefit. Meditation to determine blocks and areas of stagnation in life is useful now, and the end result can mean a release of dammed-up life force that can be utilised, thus bringing us more strength. It is also a time for spiritual work, scrying, and any meaningful inner effort. This is not a wasted period, but a necessary one, as preparation for the approaching expansive cycle when sun and moon conjoin once more and begin a new phase. Much can be accomplished by working with the energies instead of falling into sluggish resistance, and doing so will dispel the weariness that people often experience now, and will bring satisfaction and a sense of completion.

OLD MOON MEDITATION

You should do this meditation at night, when the moon has vanished to its pre-new, dark state. Burn a sombre incense such as Hecate or myrrh. One can be made up by adding several drops of patchouli oil to a small jar of myrrh resin and stirring thoroughly. Don't light the point candles, but instead use one black candle on the altar. Cast your circle in the usual manner.

Make yourself comfortable by sitting on a cushion, meditation stool, or chair within easy reach of the altar. Make sure you have matches or a lighter near you. Ask the Goddess in her Crone form to protect and guide you. Concentrate on the candle flame for a while, allowing yourself to relax, letting your breathing become deeper till you can feel that both breath and vital energy are rooted into your lower stomach area. Feel the weight of your body, your legs, and the point of contact between your buttocks and the surface on which you are seated. Let everything go so that your back is straight and yet you seem to be settled into your thighs and posterior, and by extension into the floor and the earth beneath.

When you are feeling relaxed and stable, snuff out the candle, close your eyes, and begin to turn your attention inward, withdrawing interest from your surroundings and focussing on your personal inner realm.

If this seems difficult at first, concentrate on your stomach area while taking a few very deep breaths and imagining that your whole body is comfortably swelling till it is like a huge room with you inside.

Once you feel you have gone into yourself, gently explore what you find there. Tell yourself that you will only see whatever is safe and productive for you to view. Ask the Goddess to help you. Go in peace, and tread softly through your own inner process. Keep sitting there, keep exploring inwardly bit by bit until feelings, thoughts, or images begin to arise, and when they do, view them in a relaxed and slightly detached manner, allowing them to unfold without forcing the issue at all. Imagine, if you like, that you are in a large attic with many dusty lumps under sheets and in boxes. Some of these may attract you, may even light up so that you are persuaded to look into them. Lift the covers on the ones that you instinctively feel are relevant to you. Or if you prefer, visualise your inner space as a cave, a hollow, or a chamber deep in the earth where leaves and soil go through the process of breakdown and regeneration and where treasures are buried. Whatever comes out of this meditation, whatever you perceive or experience, the idea is that you will be able to release or transform what you find so that you can clear space or liberate energy. Many of the blocks that we experience in our lives are caused by pockets of dammed-up energy that can be confronted and let go of, leaving us unburdened and refreshed. This is not meant to be a traumatic process in which you attempt to face past pain that would be better dealt with by means of professional help. Nor should you try to force yourself to let go of something that is still dear to you, no matter how much your rational mind tells you to. Be prepared for brief tears, laughter, or other powerful emotions during the resolution process. If nothing comes up at all, it doesn't matter, and you may need only to enjoy a tranquil interlude.

When you feel it is time to end the meditation, slowly bring your attention back to the surface, and begin to raise your level of breathing to your chest, then your throat, quickening its rhythm as you do so. Then clap your hands briskly but not too hard, relight the candle, stretch your limbs, and look around.

The four goddesses particularly appropriate for the old moon are the Greek goddess Hecate, the Celtic goddess Cerridwen, Inanna, and Kali, the Indian goddess of destruction. God forms who can be worked with are Anubis, who is the Egyptian guide of the souls of the dead, and the European Horned God Cernunnos, who culls the sick and wounded but guards the animals.

CERRIDWEN

Although I have called her Celtic, Cerridwen is probably extremely ancient, possibly even Neolithic, and is a deity of death and regeneration, as well as being the Mother of the corn and of fertility. Her cauldron stands for the forces of dissolution and new growth that are found throughout life and especially in the seasonal cycle. Cerridwen has qualities of wisdom but can also be perceived as being somewhat shamanic, as is seen in the legend wherein she changes into one animal after another in order to pursue Gwion. Her sacred animal is the white sow: the pig is often found in mythical association with the Goddess, especially in her chthonic or Underworld role.

In Welsh myth, Cerridwen had a child who was dark and ugly, so she decided to boil up a magical brew in her cauldron, which would give him compensatory gifts of wisdom and prophecy. She instructed a little boy, Gwion, to stir the potion while she slept, but he splashed three drops on to his thumb, which he then put in his mouth to ease the burn. Of course, by doing this he ingested some of the potion, which gave him magical powers. Cerridwen woke up, and when she discovered what had happened she furiously attacked Gwion, who fled. Thanks to the magic brew, he was able to change himself into a hare, but Cerridwen became a hound and gave chase; then Gwion became a bird, but Cerridwen transformed into a hawk; then she was an otter to Gwion's fish. At last, exhausted, Gwion changed into an ear of corn and hid on the threshing floor, but Cerridwen became a black hen and ate him. Within her womb he stayed nine months and was born to her as a beautiful baby, Taliesin. Cerridwen was unable to bring herself to murder such a beautiful child, and so threw him into the river wrapped in a leather bag. He was found and rescued and went on to become the wisest and most gifted of bards.

In this legend can be seen the transformation of dark to light, of something considered ugly or deficient into fresh, radiant growth. Thus Cerridwen can be worked with at old moon when something needs to be transformed or transmuted so that it can be put to creative use. The tale, like many Celtic stories, deals with the fact that the things we often think are hideous or warped are often filled with hidden beauty and potential.

HECATE

Hecate is a goddess of death and of the forces of regeneration and rebirth, and this is seen in the dual role she played in Greek religion. Her daytime self was a fertility goddess, keeper of the crops and of agriculture in general, and also a goddess of birth. By night she was associated with tombs, burial places, and crossroads, and was often allied with witches and magic. She was portrayed by the ancient Greeks as being triple headed, showing her rulership over birth, death, and growth, and the three major phases of the moon, wherein she most definitely plays the part of the lovely Maiden, bringer of birth, and of the Crone. She has links with dogs, the serpent, horses, pigs, frogs, and the lion, and is accompanied by hounds, as is Artemis (with whom she is linked). Hecate is a chthonic goddess, and as such is appropriate for the dark moon. The willow tree is sacred to her, as are cypress and yew, the latter being a tree of regeneration that grows afresh from its own dying trunk. Cypress and yew both grow in graveyards. Hecate's dual associations of night and day make her a deity of both dark and light and, therefore, of the transformation of one into the other. She can be given offerings of dark honey, dried figs, grain, and pomegranates.

Hecate Meditation

This meditation also is intended to be done at dark of moon, before the astrological new moon. Sit in a dim and quiet place where you will be comfortable. If you can do this meditation outside at night it would be ideal, but otherwise in your personal ritual space is fine. Don't worry about candles, and only use incense if you really feel it would add to the meditation experience, in which case one of the fragrances mentioned earlier in the chapter will do. Settle into comfortable, rhythmic deep breathing so you become gradually more and more relaxed while retaining an alertness (keeping your spine straight but not rigid will help). Close your eyes.

When you have breathed deeply for about ten cycles of in and out, relaxing more with each outward breath, you will begin to be aware of surroundings and sensations different from those of the place your physical self occupies . . . beginning with a sense of space around you. Feel of tussocky grass is beneath you. It is night, very still and dark, though some stars are visible. There is no moon. You can tell by the vague outlines of low mounds that you are in an ancient burial place, but you do not find this thought disturbing—indeed there is a feeling of hush and peace, though it has a potent edge that you are unable to describe. A faint breeze arises, bringing you the distant sound of some night creature that at first you take to be a screech owl, though as the sound comes a little nearer it suggests the howl of a hound. There is a bitter, resinous scent that may be cypress or myrrh, or a blend of sombre evergreens. As your eyes become accustomed to the light, you can see that there is some kind of rock-framed entrance in one of the mounds, directly opposite where you are sitting, and this is flanked on the left by a large willow, trunk broken but sprouting with new branches. To the right is a massive yew tree, trunk cracked and rotted, but with a vigorous growth of upward sweeping branches and fringed, greenish-black leaves.

As you watch the mysterious entrance before you, a glow appears from its depths, flickering and dancing, resolving itself into the light of flames that approach the rocky gateway, casting light higher and higher. A woman emerges carrying a burning torch in each hand, and by this lurid glow you can just make out her face and the fact that she is robed, though her features seem to shift and transform in the inconstant light so that at one moment she appears young and beautiful, and at the next ancient, eye sockets hollowed by living shadows. Her countenance is stern. A dark, slinking form near her startles you, but the click of claws gives a clue to its canine identity.

As the woman approaches, the torchlight dazzles you, but you feel hard, dry fingers grasp yours and help you to rise to your feet. You follow her guiding hand. After a little way of walking, she pushes the flaming brands into the ground and steps back beyond their light, but you sense that she has not withdrawn completely and still watches you from just beyond the periphery of your vision. She has not spoken a word, and yet you know that some sort of communication is going on whereby she probes your mind, questioning, and you respond from some unfathomable part of yourself that bypasses conscious thought. Your senses seem to come alive so that the brush of displaced air on your skin is like the rasp of roughened silk; you can smell soil and damp mulched leaves so acutely that the odours leave a taste on your tongue; the whisper of night creatures and the gentle sough of an intermittent breeze are like a symphony of sound that connects you to earth and stars and the fathomless depths above and beneath you. The torches' red and fading glow reveals that you are standing at a crossroads where grass and stones and beaten turf meet. It is as though you wait at the pivotal point round which all the worlds revolve.

From a place inside you, beyond your perception till now, arise mingled joy and pain, weariness, enthusiasm, certainty, directness, and doubt. All wash through you in a flood that leaves you empty yet at peace. You see that the crossroads represents your own life, the point of decision from which you can choose your direction and purpose now that past issues that had held you back have surfaced and are resolved. You do not have to make that decision now, but instead will hold this place inside your heart, knowing that when events in the outer world trigger the choice, you will know what to do.

The torches have burned right out and a freshening wind scatters their embers, leaving you in darkness once more. Take ten breaths, breathing in an increasingly shallow and rapid manner. At the tenth breath you will feel alert and aware. The goddess has left. The scene around you has vanished and you are increasingly conscious of the sense of being in the outer world place in which you began the meditation. Open your eyes and reorientate so that you connect with your waking self. Get up, stretch, and go to find something to eat and drink, then write about your experiences.

Hecate can be approached when you need help to remove some obstacle or to release old conditions and bring in the new. Ask respectfully and she will treat you with fairness and love. Demand from her without deference and she will take you on a whirlwind journey that leaves you shaken and infinitely more humble and wise.

KALI

This Indian goddess is the dark, devouring aspect of the Great Mother. She is the darker side of Shiva, and together they dance the universe in and out of manifestation. Kali's imagery makes her seem very fearsome: she is naked but for a girdle of severed human heads, a necklace of skulls, and a tiger skin cloak. Her tongue lolls out of her mouth, her eyes are fiery red, and she has a prominent third eye in the middle of her brow. To this day goats (and, secretly, children too) are sacrificed to her in India to satisfy her lust for blood. However, Kali stands for the destruction that is necessary in order for new things to come into being. Two of her hands hold weapons, but the other two are raised in blessing, showing that beneficence can arise from dissolution. It is probably better not to work directly with Kali, as she is such a powerful force, but she can be acknowledged at old moon and thanked for the part she plays in removing stale conditions that would otherwise slow down progress and mire our lives. She represents the shocking bolt from the blue that turns our lives upside down but clears the way for a better phase. Sometimes she can represent that part of ourselves that we are afraid to face, which we think will consume us if we allow ourselves to acknowledge it, and yet which liberates us and frees up useful power once we bring it into the light of day.

INANNA

This Sumerian goddess has been described already in the new moon section of this book. In the legend of her descent, she went down to the Underworld to confront her sister Ereshkigal, hoping to challenge her and win her kingdom. She had to pass through seven gates, a symbolic passage through seven levels of consciousness, or being, to the inner self. At the first gate she had to remove her crown, emblem of authority in the outer world. At the second gate her earrings were removed. At the third gate she took off her necklace. At the fourth gate her breastplate was removed. At the fifth she untied her girdle. At the sixth gate she took off her anklets and bangles. Finally, at the seventh gate, her veil, or cloak, was removed, leaving her without any kind of protection or adornment. Because of this descent to the Underworld, where she underwent a total stripping away of everything that defined her persona, being left naked and vulnerable, yet emerging whole and renewed at the end of three days, she can be called upon for help at the very end of the moon's cycle, when you may want to shed outworn factors in your life. Whenever something is released from the psyche, there is a temporary feeling of emptiness and vulnerability that is uncomfortable, but is a necessary part of the process of letting go. Inanna can help us to confront this emptiness and find ways to move forward to the regeneration process that prepares us for fresh cycles of growth and productivity.

Light dark red candles for Inanna at this time in the lunar round, and ask her to help you to examine your life for anything that is blocking progress or causing stagnation or pain. The following is an invocation to her that can be used at dark moon, before the time of astrological new moon arrives:

Fertile goddess, Warrior Queen, Star of Morning,
you trod this route before me and understand my pain.
I have gone down into darkness and am empty and alone.
Take my hand and give me courage to face my own truth.
Lead me into the light of a fresh day.

ANUBIS

Anubis is the jackal-headed god of the dead from Ancient Egypt. Jackals have associations with graveyards and places of burial. Sometimes Anubis is seen as a man with a jackal's head and sometimes as the beast itself. His job was to supervise the process of mummification, and he is black because that is the colour that embalmed corpses turn. The priest presiding over the process of embalming would wear a mask in the form of a head of Anubis. He was originally the god of the Underworld, but Osiris took his place in later Egyptian dynasties, relegating Anubis to the assistant who led the deceased to the Halls of Judgment and helped to weigh each heart against the feather of Maat. His direction is west, which was the gateway to death in the Egyptian as well as the Celtic cultures. He guides the soul not only in death but in sleep, guarding it so that no harm will come to it. When the Hellenic culture came to Egypt, Anubis was associated with the god Hermes, who has similar attributes.

This profound and protective god form can be called upon when you want to let go of a phase of your life and move on to something else. Burn a frankincense and myrrh mixture and ask him to help you to determine what you need to let go of, then release the old willingly and lovingly and ask for his guidance in finding your new direction. He is strongly linked with death and rebirth on every level. Ask for his protection and guidance when you are making a transition from one phase of life to the next.

CERNUNNOS

This is the antlered god of ancient Europe, beloved of present-day pagans. He is lord of life and death, the keeper of the wild herds who culls the sick and dying but protects all wild creatures. At Samhain, he guards the Gates of Death so that departed souls might return to be with their loved ones in the world of the living for a brief while. At old moon and dark of moon he is seen as the wise old partner of the Crone, and can be called on in rituals at this time.

SOME MAGIC APPROPRIATE FOR THE OLD MOON

• When the last quarter has gone by, write the name of something you wish to decrease (for example, poverty) on to the side of a black candle and burn it every night until the new moon. Be careful to state that nobody, including yourself, is to be harmed by your magic and that you don't want to lose anything you hold dear.

• If you want to cleanse an athame or other magical equipment, bury it in dry compost or earth in your cauldron for the last three days of the moon's cycle. Say, "Dark mother, make this clean again." The earth will draw out negativity. Scatter the earth in the garden afterward and ask for the Mother to purify it.

• When you wish to release yourself from an unwanted condition, such as illness or tiredness, cast a circle and then take a black candle and concentrate on imbuing it with the energy of the thing to be eliminated. Then leave the candle (in a holder) burning in a container of water—the water should cover only the last inch or so of the candle base. When the flame burns down as far as the water and is extinguished by it, the condition will be gone. Pour the water down the sink or toilet and ask for it to be cleansed of all harm before it goes back into the system. You should now feel cleansed and released from the former burden.

• If you wish to be rid of something (not people . . . please!), then after the full moon take a length of black cord or ribbon and tie seven knots into it, imagining as you do so that each knot secures the unwanted part of your life so that it leaves you and is contained in the cord. Seven days before new moon, go outside after dark and untie one knot, shaking out the cord and letting the energy tied into it fly off into the air, to be scattered harmlessly to the four winds and the four quarters. Do the same thing for the next six nights. Whatever you wanted to banish will now be gone forever. With this, as with any banishing, think of something new and productive to fill the gap left in your life.

- Leave the altar bare of flowers, or let the ones from previous rituals remain, gradually decaying.

- Burn black, dark purple, dark red, green, or very dark blue candles, or no candles at all.

- Use sombre smelling incense such as patchouli, myrrh, Hecate, or a mixture with a few drops of cypress oil added.

- Raise energy with slow drumming or chanting, or keep the rite low-key and don't raise any at all.

- Call on the Goddess as the Wise Old Woman, the Grandmother, the Hag or the Crone, or as Hecate, Cerridwen, Kali, the Cailleagh, or any other dark goddess.

- Use old moon energies for magic of elimination or banishing, or for spells involving the death and regeneration of something.

- For the feast, have red grape juice or wine, and a dark food such as rye bread, or flapjacks made with molasses and honey, the recipe for which is given below.

Honey and Molasses Flapjacks

This recipe makes dark, rich-tasting flapjacks that are full of iron and other minerals. They are delicious, but an acquired taste if you are used to using only refined white sugar.

2½ tablespoons margarine or butter
1 tablespoon dark runny honey
1 tablespoon molasses or black treacle
6 rounded tablespoons rolled oats

Preheat oven to gas mark 5/190°C/375°F. Lightly grease a shallow baking pan or cake tin. Melt the margarine in a large saucepan over a medium heat. Add the honey and molasses, and allow them to melt into the margarine. When mixture comes to a rolling boil, turn off the heat. Add the oats and stir till thoroughly mixed. Spoon mixture into the center of the baking pan or cake tin and shape into a circle. Bake in the middle of the oven for ten minutes or until brown. Cool for a few minutes, then cut into slices or segments. Makes one seven-inch round flapjack.

OLD MOON BANISHING RITUAL

This rite is intended for two or more people, but it can be adapted for a solitary by sending the anticlockwise (or widdershins) energy into a black candle and then burning it till it is gone.

- Light the point candles and altar candles, and cast the circle in the usual way.

- Leave the altar bare of flowers.

- Call on the Goddess as the Crone.

- Hold hands and imagine raising a tall column of energy in the closed circle of your linked hands. One way to do this is to breathe out energy on your outward exhalations and "see" it building the energy column higher and higher.

- Let each person state what he wants to eliminate from his life, and each person present should concentrate on the voiced wishes. You can go round the circle up to three times, but don't try to banish more than that or you will overload the ritual.

- When all is spoken, begin to slowly push the energy downward and anticlockwise with your minds, and as you do so visualise the factors to be eliminated and see them being woven into the column of energy. See the energy with all your debris slowly subsiding until it is a dark, oily puddle, and then a swirling, glugging sinkhole that eventually soaks into the ground. Ask the earth to take it and cleanse it so that it can be regenerated and used positively somewhere in the future.

- When the whirlpool of dark, murky energy has gone, release each other's hands.

- Now state one positive thing for each of the things banished and resolve to work on them when the new moon comes.

- End the circle as you normally would after cakes and wine.

As the darkest point in the moon's cycle approaches, all life seems to have been leached out of existence and everything is flat, dull, and weary. But this period lasts a very short time. The dark moon bridges the transition between old and new, when the cycle will commence once more.

the moon in astrological signs

Although the full moon can be used for any appropriate magic, sometimes it is useful to time a working for when she falls in an astrological sign compatible with the type of result you wish to obtain. This concept can be applied to other phases as well, but the astrological placement of the full moon is easy to determine, as it falls in the sign opposite that occupied by the sun; for example, if the sun is in Virgo, then the full moon will be in Pisces since they are 180 degrees apart at this time. The sign the sun occupies, as well as the day of the week and the time of the year, will affect your work, but the sign the moon is in will be the most important and determining factor. The following is a list of the twelve zodiac signs and the type of magical work and activities that might be done. I have given the colour correspondences for each, as these can be used in place of the usual ones if desired. Be aware too that the moon's power will marry to a certain extent with the vibrations of the planet ruling the astrological sign it is in, thus colouring your results to some degree. These ruling planets are also given at the end of each section. But don't feel bound or inhibited by astrological factors. The moon's phase itself is the prime ingredient to consider with occult activity.

FULL MOON IN ARIES

Work with the Aries full moon when you want to bring a lot of energy and enthusiasm to what you are planning, or when you want rapid success in a new venture. Be careful to word your spells meticulously, with attention to the goal and motivation, as Aries can be a bit selfish, and it's easy to get so carried away by its power that you forget to consider the rights of others. Arian energy is extremely competitive. Athletic or other sporting skills can be helped along with magic that is done on this moon, though the results will assist you with the necessary hard work that goes into training rather than confer instant victory.

Colour(s) to use for candles, cords, et cetera: red

Suggested incense: cinnamon

Ruling planet: Mars

FULL MOON IN TAURUS

Prosperity spells can work fantastically well with the waxing or full moon in Taurus, as it is the earthiest of the signs and very much concerned with materialism. It's also appropriate for gaining the confidence to speak out, especially publicly, as Taurus rules the throat, that part of the body and auric field closely related with speech and self-expression. Work on the Taurus full moon for growth of any kind as well, including cultivating a garden or tending metaphorical or physical crops. It can also be good for bringing the money to enjoy the good things of life when you are badly in need of a break. Don't forget to work for needs and reasonable wants. Taurus energy can encourage greed and hedonism if you aren't careful. Great staying power is possible with the help of Taurus, so it can be channelled to you so you can stick to something or see a difficult situation through to the end if it is preferable to do so. This is one of the signs helpful for bringing a lover into your life, and can attract a very sensuous love affair.

Colour(s) to use for candles, cords, et cetera: pale to medium blue; green; pink; rose; mauve; burnt orange

Ruling planet: Venus

Suggested incense: benzoin

FULL MOON IN GEMINI

If you want the opportunity for short-distance travel, then magic done on this moon is ideal. It fosters all kinds of business communication as well, and would be the best time to try to ensure that any deals and transactions entered into or contracts signed will be to your advantage and will not deceive you in some way. This is also the moon to work with if you want to be successful with learning something new (for example, learning a language), and especially with information technology (IT) skills and computing. Disputes with neighbours or communication problems with brothers and sisters can be successfully sorted out now as well.

Colour(s) to use for candles, cords, et cetera: blue; yellow; violet

Suggested incense: lavender

Ruling planet: Mercury

FULL MOON IN CANCER

This moon is concerned with family, the home, and motherhood. A spell to get pregnant would have a better chance of bearing fruit at this time, as would one to find a new home. Exploration of previous lives also ties in with Cancer's links with tradition and the past. Scrying or other divination will be especially rewarding when the moon is in Cancer, as it is a naturally psychic and receptive sign. It relates to the Mother phase of the Goddess, who can be appealed to now for help and support. Use Cancer's acquisitive streak to bring in anything you want for your environment, such as old and tasteful artefacts, magical tools and altar decorations, god and goddess images, and so forth.

Colour(s) to use for candles, cords, et cetera: white; silver

Suggested incense: damiana

Ruling planet: the moon

FULL MOON IN LEO

Leo full moon is ideal for male virility and fertility spells. It also fosters confidence, courage, strength, and leadership abilities, so if you feel you are lacking in any of these areas, then this is the optimum time to work to build them up or increase them. Magic to bring a large sum of necessary money can be done now, and is very likely to succeed—though only if it is really badly needed. Trying to acquire wealth for self-indulgent purposes will probably fail because of the lack of urgency and, therefore, insufficient motivation. Remember, you need to be passionate about the outcome to work successful magic.

Colour(s) to use for candles, cords, et cetera: gold; deep sunny yellow; radiant orange

Suggested incense: frankincense

Ruling planet: the sun

FULL MOON IN VIRGO

Virgo energy is good for magical work involving health, going on a fitness regime, refining the diet, getting into vegetarian or whole-food diets, and so on. In fact, it is good for healing and purification generally, and for healing animals in particular. Spells for acquiring or improving skills, especially relating to handicrafts and other manual abilities, are especially appropriate to this sign. Virgo teaches us to take care of the details, so tuning into its essence and using it in magic can be helpful if you have a tendency to spoil things through oversight or skimping. Virgo is the sign of the harvest, and magic can be done now to ensure a productive harvest from any viable enterprise.

Colour(s) to use for candles, cords, et cetera: grey; green; black

Suggested incense: lemongrass

Ruling planet: Mercury

FULL MOON IN LIBRA

Work on partnerships when the moon is in this sign, especially if you want to bring a sense of balance and harmony into your relationships. Marriage and other legal partnerships, such as business contracts and agreements, come under Libra. This is the time to concentrate on legal matters too, and to send power toward seeing that justice is done. You can also jump-start a flagging social life by magic done during the Libra full moon, though be aware that the results may manifest as having a good time, dressing up, or wining and dining rather than forming deep friendships. You can work for attracting love into your life now.

Colour(s) to use for candles, cords, et cetera: pink; rose; pale green; mauve; powder blue

Suggested incense: rose

Ruling planet: Venus

FULL MOON IN SCORPIO

During the Scorpio full moon, work on matters requiring insight, as Scorpio helps us to get to the bottom of things and to analyse what makes them the way they are. Spells to help learn about the occult or psychology will be especially successful now. Scorpio is a very sexual sign, so if you want to increase your libido or attract a passionate love affair, then this is the time, though be aware that relationships that begin with a Scorpio influence will probably be transformational—and the process will not always be comfortable or predictable. This is also an astrological position concerned with healing, especially of the mind and emotions. Scrying now will bring profound and sometimes disturbing results. If you want to make sure that some personal matter stays secret, then do a spell for it now. Scorpio also gives superior powers of concentration or single-mindedness, both of which might be necessary in some situations, as perhaps when studying or staying with a task.

Colour(s) to use for candles, cords, et cetera: deep red

Suggested incense: kyphi

Ruling planet: Pluto (dual rulership with Mars)

FULL MOON IN SAGITTARIUS

Long-distance travel relates to Sagittarius, so the full moon here will be useful for work aimed at making long journeys possible, or for bringing protection during them. All kinds of study and learning can be helped by magical work that uses the energies of full moon in Sagittarius, as can writing and publishing—in fact, if you want to send a book to a publisher in the hope of having it accepted, then magic done now will boost its chances. Sagittarius is concerned with religion and philosophy, and with spiritual seeking in general, so it is appropriate for workings that help you decide about connected issues or even with embarking on a new soul path. Lastly, like Aries, Sagittarius can help develop sporting prowess, though it is not as competitive as the former sign.

Colour(s) to use for candles, cords, et cetera: purple; royal blue

Suggested incense: cedar wood

Ruling planet: Jupiter

FULL MOON IN CAPRICORN

Spells for working on career matters are helped by the Capricorn full moon, especially those involving the prospect of great success or a rise to the top. Capricorn can be very ambitious, and so its powers can bolster flagging determination. However, this is also a deeply spiritual sign and can help with matters surrounding initiation. If you need help getting organised in some area of your life, then this too can benefit from Capricornian magical work, but beware of being too bossy as a result!

Colour(s) to use for candles, cords, et cetera: black; dark green; dark blue; indigo

Suggested incense: myrrh

Ruling planet: Saturn

FULL MOON IN AQUARIUS

Anything scientific or technological responds well to this airy astrological sign, and so full moon work now can be very helpful. It's good for forming or maintaining friendships too, as well as establishing groups. If you want a spell to help you gain more freedom or autonomy in a situation, then work magically for it while the moon is in Aquarius, though be very careful with wording, as Aquarian tendencies can be rebellious if not downright anarchic. It's also good to channel Aquarian power if you want help with becoming more detached, or as an antidote to being overemotional. You can also foster the development of intuition now, or increase it. Studying astrology can be very fulfilling if begun when the waxing or full moon is in Aquarius.

Colour(s) to use for candles, cords, et cetera: electric blue

Suggested incense: eucalyptus

Ruling planet: Uranus (dual rulership with Saturn)

FULL MOON IN PISCES

Work now to help with creativity, especially with music, poetry, or art. Pisces is extremely caring and compassionate, so its energies can be used to either become more understanding and empathetic or to direct those qualities toward yourself. This is also a prime time for all kinds of prayer or meditation, as Pisces helps us to lose ourselves in the infinite . . . it is devotional. Its energies help to enhance or develop psychic powers, especially clairvoyance. This is also a time when it is easier to allow life to flow rather than forcing some issue, so you might want to use the full moon in Pisces to drift, dream, and see what imaginative ideas develop.

Colour(s) to use for candles, cords, et cetera: sea green; sea blue;
   misty grey; pearly mauves and blues

Suggested incense: sage

Ruling planet: Neptune (dual rulership with Jupiter)

Working with the astrological moons can be productive and rewarding. If you find you gain satisfactory results, in keeping with the purpose toward which your magic was directed, then it might be useful to research this subject in more depth. Astrological workings can be pinned down to days of the week and even planetary hours so that a really comprehensive spell would incorporate these in conjunction with the appropriate moon's phase and the correct time of year (Yule to Midsummer for increase, and Summer Solstice to Midwinter for decrease or inward work).

One last point: When determining the sign the moon occupies, you really need to look it up in an accurate ephemeris. The moon sometimes changes signs during a twenty-four hour period, and calendars, diaries, and almanacs often give only the position for midday or midnight.

the celtic tree calendar

A lunar system very popular among modern witches and other pagans is the Celtic Tree Calendar, which provides a means of following the lunar changes in the year's energies as well as the solar ones. The thirteen trees are loosely tied to the thirteen moons we experience each year, and each tree moon encompasses more or less one or two astrological signs—though this needs to be checked for individual years, as the timing of new moons is not precisely the same each year. Some tree moons fall near one of the eight festivals of the Wheel of the Year, and, therefore, take on some of the qualities of that festival. I have described here the so-called *Beth, Luis, Nuin* calendar that starts with the new moon nearest the Winter Solstice and runs till the next new moon, and so on round the twelve-month solar year. The other tree calendar in use commences at Samhain. Each lunar cycle, from new moon to the next new moon, will carry the flavour of the tree that rules it, and this will colour that time period with its essence, and will theoretically influence anyone born then, much as the sun signs do.

Be aware that the various versions of the Celtic Tree Calendar may not be genuinely ancient, though there is no way of knowing for sure. Modern pagans have tended to romanticise Celtic life, lore, and customs so that many things are attributed to them, and have become a part of modern pagan practice, but these things may never have happened at all, or may have been of minor importance. There are some anomalies as well; for instance, I have always associated hawthorn with Beltane—after all, that's when we bring in the May, the magical blossom of the hawthorn—yet the Celtic Tree Calendar gives willow for this festival. However, whether its roots are genuinely ancient or not is far less important than whether something works or has meaning to practitioners adopting it.

The tree calendar is also loosely affiliated with the ogham alphabet, which may be extremely ancient, though most examples, carved on large stones, are later than A.D. 300 or A.D. 400. Ogham is an alphabet based on a series of cross-hatched lines, and each letter relates to a tree and is thought to convey the qualities of that tree. There are many theories about its historical use, some adhered to by modern Celtic and Druidic groups. The ogham definitely unlocks certain energies if used as a meditation device, and these can be employed as a cipher to understand the trees concerned. It is also used as a system of divination. If you are attracted to ogham, it is worth researching it and meditating on it yourself. This is what I have done with the specific trees in the tree calendar, and I give the results below, along with descriptions of the trees as found in their natural habitat.

BIRCH

Celtic name: Beth

Associated festival: Winter Solstice

Description of the tree: A slender, graceful tree with small serrated drop-shaped leaves that turn golden yellow in autumn. It bears long catkins in spring. The bark of mature birches is patched black and white and has a loose, peeling appearance because the tree sheds the old layer of skin as it renews its protective surface. However, birch saplings have reddish-brown splotches instead of black on the trunks. Birches often grow at the edge of woods, being the first to sprout up on new ground, breaking down the soil so that less hardy strains can spread out and thrive later. Although they are supposed to live only about fifty years, in fact some survive longer, growing into fabulously gnarled and twisted specimens.

Qualities: Inception; fertility; conception; birth or rebirth; cleansing; purification; creativity; young children. Birch was once used to beat the boundaries of parishes. It was historically used as a cane for purification by chastisement. Birch twigs are used to whip up the circulation after a hot bath to rid the system of impurities via the skin. The twigs are also the traditional basis of the brush part of the witches' besom or broom, and play a part in removing astral debris from the circle's edge. Birch is also connected with shamanism. It is a sociable, "chatty" tree that quickly responds to human presence. I once worked in a school that had birches planted all over the campus, and the trees thrived on having young people around, what with all the activity and interchange that that entailed.

ROWAN (MOUNTAIN ASH)

Celtic name: Luis

Associated festival: Imbolc

Description of the tree: Very slender and delicate looking with long leaves growing on either side of central spines. In spring it has a froth of tiny creamy white blossoms. By autumn the flowers will have become bright red berries, much loved by birds, and the leaves turn a fiery orange. Rowan belongs to the apple family, as you can see if you cut across one of the berries horizontally, as a tiny pentagram-shaped seed container will be revealed, much like a miniature version of the one found inside an apple.

Qualities: Protection; magic; initiation. Rowan was once planted near the back door of cottages to guard against witches! This may come from the fact that it is a protector against enchantment, and witches of old were reputed to be enchanters. Rowan trees are thought to guard sacred gateways into the Otherworld. Leafy rowan twigs bound with red ribbon were placed in stables and biers to protect the livestock. Rowan has a special, magical feeling energy and makes good wands for occult work, though the wood is difficult to work with because it is quite hard.

ASH

Celtic name: Nuin

Description of the tree: Ash has a straight grey trunk that is silvery coloured when the tree is young, but darkens with age. Its leaves are a similar shape to those of the rowan, opening from black buds in spring. The flowers are pinkish-purple and become winged seedlike fruits rather like those of the sycamore. When the wood is cut, it exudes a reddish sap that makes the tree look as if it is bleeding. The ground beneath ash is usually quite bare, as these trees alter the composition of the soil so that very little is able to grow near them.

Qualities: Ash is the Norse World Tree, Yggdrasil, with roots in the Underworld, trunk on the earthly level of being, and upper branches in the heavens amid the stars. Ash is supposed to have qualities of great wisdom, and to confer a sense of spiritual knowledge and a comprehension of the unity of existence when pieces of the wood are carried or when it is meditated upon. It is the wood preferred for the shaft of a witch's broom stick. It makes powerful wands that can be used when determination is needed to ensure the success of a spell.

ALDER

Celtic name: Fearn

Description of the tree: Alder looks very similar to birch, though the trunks are yellowy-grey and the leaves are rounder. The long, densely formed catkins transform into toothed, black, conelike fruits. Alder grows near water, especially rivers.

Qualities: Alder stands for defence and protection, yet it has a watery, intuitive side as well. It can bring spiritual perception won by standing up for your beliefs and following through on hunches. The tree is linked with Bran the Blessed of Ancient Celtic times, and his bird, the raven. Because its wood is quite waterproof, alder was often used historically for the foundations of dwellings where flooding or a rising water level was a risk, and many European cathedrals had alder piles placed under their foundations to shore them up. Although it is so similar to birch, alder has a more serious character and lacks the happy, bright feel of birch.

WILLOW

Celtic name: Salle

Description of the tree: The traditional willow is not the famous weeping variety, but white willow or crack willow. Both of the latter have straighter trunks and a denser appearance than the weeping willow. Crack willow is so called because the trunk cracks or splits when it reaches a certain size, though the tree continues to grow afterward. Willows often thrive along river banks, where their branches and leaves trail in the water. The leaves themselves are extremely long and narrow, and are silvery underneath. They turn through every shade of yellow and brown in the autumn, from lemon to deep chocolate. White willow has tooth-edged leaves, while those of crack willow are smooth. Willow is so tenacious that cut branches will sprout afresh and will root themselves if left lying on the ground. If you build a fence with willow staves, you are likely to wind up with a hedge!

Qualities: Feminine cycles of fertility; emotion; clairvoyance; intuition; magic. This tree is concerned with lunar work. Meditating on willow will often release bottled-up emotions. Willow wands are ideal for female witches, and the wood is soft enough to be easily carved with decorative symbols or patterns. Pliable willow branches are often used in basket making. Meditating on willow brings a sense of deep connection to the Goddess.

HAWTHORN (WHITETHORN)

Celtic name: Huath

Associated festival: Beltane—although willow coincides with the chrono-
logical time of Beltane, hawthorn is the tree that symbolises the May
festival.

Description of the tree: Although hawthorn can grow to a fair height, it is
usually seen as a small tree or shrub. Its twisty, tangled branches,
dense foliage, and sharp thorns make it an impenetrable hedge
plant, and it is often seen along roadside verges or in the hedgerows
between fields. The trunk and branches are silvery brown and the
leaves consist of three or more bulbous lobes with deep indentations
between them, and the edges are serrated. The sprays of foamy,
cream coloured blossom change into clusters of ruby-red berries by
autumn. The flowers have a powerful, heady fragrance that some
people have likened to the smell of female sexuality.

Qualities: Protection; fertility; cleansing and purification; healing.
Hawthorn is a magical-feeling tree often associated with the fairy
folk. Its fresh, pretty greenery in early summer seems to generate a
mystical atmosphere that makes one want to crawl under its
branches and somehow enter an otherworldly place. Over the centuries, hawthorn has become linked with chastity, which is strange
because it is deeply symbolic of Beltane and May Morning, being
the bridal wreath of the Goddess, and after the uninhibited sexuality of May Eve, people would bring its blossom into their homes—
the only time of the year when it was not considered unlucky to
do so. Meditating on hawthorn can help to release old pain and
repressed trauma from the auric field, and I have used it for this
purpose, though the shock of release was briefly jolting and
uncomfortable before resolving into a sense of relief. Places where
hawthorn grows profusely often seem to mediate earth energies
and evoke a connection to ancient times when people were more
in tune with the land.

OAK

Celtic name: Duir

Associated festival: Summer Solstice

Description of the tree: Oaks are massive when mature, with wide girthed trunks, and live for centuries if they survive their precarious beginnings (the young saplings are quite vulnerable because they grow so slowly, and only a few escape browsing animals or overcrowding from other trees). They are the last to leaf and the last to lose their leaves. Their ridged, rough bark is a home to many crawling insects, and their densely foliaged crowns harbour many species of beetles and winged creatures. Oak leaves are wavy edged and long, reminiscent of broadened deer antlers, and are bronze-green in spring, turning russet in autumn, by which time their feathery flowers have turned into oval shaped acorns nestled into knobbly brown cups. Oaks that grow alone have a rounded shape, with branches starting close to the ground and spreading wide. Those that have to fight for space and light in dense woodland often grow with tall, straight trunks that do not branch out till they are many feet above the ground.

Qualities: Strength; courage; endurance; fortitude; protection; fatherhood; kingship; responsibility; loyalty; the God. The oak is the door between the light and dark halves of the year, the time when the Oak King loses his battle with the Holly King, though he enjoys a brief summit to his power at Midsummer. The oaken doorway is also the gateway to other worlds of being, including the spiritual realms and the inner self. To the Druids, the oak was the King of the Forest, the most sacred of trees, and one reason they thought oaks so magical was because of their tendency to attract lightning, but also their ability to survive these lightning strikes or regenerate afterward. If you see a broken oak alone in a field, sprouting from the remaining rooted trunk, it will almost certainly have survived a lighting blast. The wood was used in times gone by to build ships, palaces, hallways, and anything that required a strong, imperishable structure.

Acorns can be dried and ground down to make a bitter tasting coffee substitute. At one time they were fed to livestock, and pigs in particular were let free to forage at the woods' edge for these fruits.

HOLLY

Celtic name: Tinne

Associated festival: Lammas

Description of the tree: Holly's prickly dark green leaves and bright red berries hardly need description, as they are famous all over the world through their association with Christmas. In spring, new acid-green leaves emerge along with tiny pink-white flowers. The holly is an evergreen, so its rounded shape remains unchanged all year round. The trunk is smooth but bears eye-shaped pits here and there in the bark, and is green in young trees but turns a silky silvery-brown with age.

Qualities: Courageous; warlike instincts; territorial; emotionally "prickly"; defensive; male sexuality. Holly represents potent male energies that can become aggressive if threatened. With its prickly leaves and upright stance, holly is always on guard. The tree yields a beautiful, white wood that darkens as it ages. Holly wands are ideal for protective magic. Holly has a very serious aura but it is deeply magical too, and holly guards the door to the inner realms, just as it watches over the way to the dark half of the year when nights grow longer and we turn inward, away from summer activity.

HAZEL

Celtic name: Coll

Description of the tree: Hazel is a shrubby tree often found in dense woodland. It is not very tall and so is popular for hedging. Its leaves are toothed and roundish, but terminate in a sharp tip. Hazel nuts, sometimes called cobs, grow in clusters with soft, leaflike cases, and turn rich russet brown when ripe.

Qualities: Wisdom; spirituality; mental alertness; quickness and agility; calculation and measurement; poetry; divination; creativity; inspiration. Hazelnuts are symbolic of encapsulated wisdom. The famous Celtic legend associated with hazel is of the salmon of wisdom taking into its watery home the hazelnuts that had fallen. Hazel wands are airy and lively feeling, and can be good when you want your magic to be very clear and to the point. Dowsing rods (used to find both water and ley energy) are usually hazel.

VINE

Celtic name: Muin

Associated festival: Mabon or Autumn Equinox

Description of the tree: This may refer to grape vines with their gnarled stems and extravagant, convoluted leaves with curling tendrils, or it may mean the blackberry, with its prickly leaves and stems and multipipped black fruits, which some sources give as the Celtic equivalent.

Qualities: Prophecy; psychic development; tenacity; unification; ecstasy. Whether blackberry or grape, the fruit associated with this lunar period can be used to make wine, and this in turn can be utilised to release inhibitions and enter a state of mind in which protective auric layers are stripped away, leaving one open to receive "messages" and impulses from beyond, and perhaps to encounter such gods as Pan and Dionysus. But this tree is also linked with harvest and with the returning of energy into the soil, so it is indicative of both the contentment of reaping the rewards of effort, and of the turning within that reveals the secrets of the soul.

IVY

Celtic name: Gort

Description of the tree: The ivy is not a tree but a climbing plant that uses other trees as its support. The leaves are a heart-shaped trefoil, the lobes a veined dark green when mature but glossy and pale when new. Ivy has a tough, fibrous stem with many hairlike roots that adhere to surfaces, digging in so that brick and stonework can be superficially damaged by them. Large trees can eventually succumb to ivy, which will smother its host. Ivy can grow in the most arid of conditions and actually prefers the shade.

Qualities: Clinging; attachment restriction; endurance; determination; euphoria. Ivy, like vine, can represent ecstatic intoxication; ivy is poisonous, but the leaves are hallucinogenic when chewed. (Don't try it . . . you may kill yourself! The dividing line between being high and being dead is quite narrow.) Because the plant can grow in the shallowest and most parched of soils, and even in cracks in walls and paving, it represents tenacity and strength against the odds. There is great wisdom in ivy too, and it is one of the plants most sacred to the Goddess, and places where ivy grows in abundance are filled with dark, enthralling mystery.

REED

Celtic name: Ngetal

Associated festival: Samhain

Appearance of the tree: This is, of course, not a tree but a grasslike plant that grows by water. It has hollow, sharp stems and is often rooted in the muddy water at the edges of rivers and lakes.

Qualities: Spiritual progress; protection and defence; hunger for truth. The sharpness of the reed is like the spears of sentinels, standing guard over our lives. At this time of year, the start of true winter, reeds can look bleak, in keeping with the death of the year and the commencement of deepest cold. Reed stands for the turning within that we often undergo now, which can nourish the inner life and give an intimation of the spiritual source for which our souls hunger.

ELDER

Celtic name: Ruis

Description of the tree: Elder is a soft wooded tree with pithy branches. The leaves are small and irregularly serrated and grow from a central spine like those of rowan or ash. The spring blooms, dish-shaped masses of rich smelling white flowerlets, become dangling bunches of purple-black berries by summer's end, and both flowers and berries are used to make wine, jams, and cordials that have a delicate flavour. The trunk of the elder is ridged and grey and the whole tree is fairly small.

Qualities: Death and regeneration; the Crone phase of the Goddess; the hag; wisdom; transformation; the Underworld. Elder has qualities of change, renewal, and rebirth. It is one of the trees associated with witches, and it is supposedly very unlucky to cut it down. Elder shows the path through the maze, the spiral path that leads within, and the meeting place where birth and death are one. An alternative tree for this time would be Yew, though this also has an affinity with Samhain, which is the Celtic New Year and the time when the dead can return in spirit form to be with those they love.

Whether the Celtic Tree Calendar is of recent origin or extremely ancient is of less importance than whether or not it works as a system. It is my personal opinion that it does work, and is very effective as a means of marking the changes in the annual cycle. If you wish to experience the energies involved for yourself, then I suggest studying the calendar from various sources, carrying small pieces of the wood of the different trees around, gathering the leaves, meditating on them, and putting samples of fruits, foliage, and twigs on your shrine so they give out their etheric essence into your environment. It would be a worthwhile exercise to study each tree as its time comes around, maybe devoting a whole month to working with it, doing visualisations and meditations and finding examples of the tree in its natural habitat.

When my husband was exploring the ogham alphabet there were trees he visited regularly. He took photos of them, drew them, sat near them so he could communicate with them and experience their personalities and qualities firsthand, and allowed his creativity to be used as a channel that flowed into poetry and art. His favourite was a large oak in the middle of woodland, off the beaten track, and he came to know the rhythm of the seasons in that place, what the tree looked like at various times of the year. Rabbits grew used to him and came quite close as he sat silently with his back against the oak's trunk, squirrels charged around in the branches above his head, and a fox used to pass by from time to time. If you feel a special affinity with one of the trees—possibly the one that is your birth tree—then you can make an extended study, observing it through the seasons and seeing how its life force ebbs and flows and how it changes visually.

The tree calendar is British in origin, but for people who live elsewhere, I would suggest experimenting with the nearest native equivalents as well as finding imported examples. It's often preferable to work with the life force already present in a place, at least at first, as doing so will mean going with rather than against the grain. The Celtic Tree Calendar is not the only one in existence; there are several other lunar calendars involving trees, and some solar ones too, and all are worth a look. However, *Beth, Luis, Nuin* is probably the most famous one, and, consequently, there should be a lot more material waiting for those who wish to study it. Working with it can help us to attune to the natural world and the influence the moon has on growth and change. (See appendix E for the ogham alphabet.)

appendix a: circle casting

The following is a basic but comprehensive circle casting ritual that can be adapted or used as it is for the moon phase work throughout the book. If you have a formula you prefer, then use it; and, likewise, embellish this one to suit your own tastes if you think it would work better for you that way. You will also need to alter it if one of the rituals given in the book asks for a different method of casting.

RITUAL BATH

A ritual bath will cleanse away the stress and negativity of daily living, relax you, and put you in the frame of mind for magical work. Look on it as a transition between everyday life and the sacred space defined by a magical circle. Putting herbs, sea salt, and/or a few drops of essential oil in the water can help, but be careful to choose fragrances that relax without sending you to sleep, and don't have the water too hot for the same reason. Try rosemary, lemon balm (be sparing or you will probably fall asleep!), lavender, vervain, mint, or flower petals such as rose. You can blend some of these together for a fragrant mix.

SETUP

You can cast the circle to include the whole of a small- to medium-sized room, though for one or two people a diameter of approximately six feet should be enough room to work comfortably.

- Put out a broom to sweep the perimeter of the circle. This preliminary method ritually cleanses the space and helps to create a meditative frame of mind.

- Decide what method you will use for raising energy, and if it will involve a drum or other instrument, make sure it is placed in the space to be used.

- You will want to have a cauldron to contain flowers or candles if the spell or rite you are going to perform needs it, and this should be put near the altar.

- Place the point or directional candles in their appropriate compass directions. Use all white candles, or yellow for east/air, red for south/fire, blue or blue-green for west/water, or green or brown for north/earth.

- Put the altar in the centre, or the north, of the circle. Place two candles, one for the Goddess and one for the God, on each side of the altar (place the Goddess candle on the left and the God candle on the right); flowers; a bowl of water; a container of salt, such as sea salt; athame and/or wand; pentacle; the censer with a fresh charcoal block inside (the censer will need to either have chains attached to suspend it or be placed on or in a safe container by which it can be carried without danger of burning you or scattering embers); incense appropriate for this particular rite; any ingredients such as candles to be used in spells; a candle snuffer and candle holders; the chalice of liquid, which will also be used for the cakes and wine ceremony; a platter with the food on it.

- Light all ritual candles, including candles for the four directions and the altar candles, but not spell candles.

- Light the incense block, then stand it on one edge so that the lit part increases more quickly.

- If you wish to sweep the circle, do so slowly and rhythmically so that it sounds relaxing, and visualise all psychic dirt being swept away.

GROUNDING AND CENTRING

This exercise releases tension, helps to ground you, and opens the chakras so that energy is flowing easily between them and can be used easily in magic.

- Stand upright with the feet slightly apart.

- Relax and begin to breathe slowly and deeply.

- Let your breath reach deeper and deeper into your body till it begins to attain its own rhythm of inward and outward breath.

- As you breathe out, begin to see any tension and anxiety leave you as a muddy grey stream flowing out through your nostrils.

- As you breathe in, visualise energising life force flowing into your lungs as golden white light.

- As you breathe, imagine your energy beginning to reach lower and lower in your body.

- Feel your feet begin to "root" into the floor and the earth beneath.

- Start to draw up bright energy so that you are both grounding yourself and replenishing your energies with earth energy.

- When you feel relaxed but wide awake, put some of your chosen incense on the charcoal.

CLEANSING WITH THE ELEMENTS

Cleansing the perimeter of the circle is done to remove any stray vibrations that might interfere with the ritual and to seal the perimeter so that the space inside is kept clean. The participant(s) should also be cleansed. The bowl of saltwater represents earth and water, and the charcoal and incense stand for fire and air, so the ritual cleansing incorporates all four basic elements.

- Put the bowl of water on the pentacle, lower the tip of your athame or wand into it, visualise a stream of cleansing light entering the water via the blade or the shaft of the wand, and say words such as:

  I cleanse and consecrate this water, that it may purify sacred space, by the power of Goddess and God.

  This removes all impurities from the water so that it can then fulfil its work of cleansing.

- The salt now needs to be blessed, though it is already pure and, unlike water, will not absorb vibrations from the atmosphere around it. The salt is needed to keep the consecrated water clean. Say:

I bless this salt, that it might protect the sacred circle, by the power of Goddess and God.

- Add three pinches of salt to the water and stir it gently in a clockwise direction.

- Begin at the northern quarter and walk slowly round the perimeter of the circle, sprinkling water as you go and visualising it as blue-white light that gently cleanses and seals the edge of the ritual space. When you have returned to the point where you started, sprinkle yourself and anyone else with you.

- Replenish the incense, then pick the censer up and carry it round the circle's edge, imagining as you do so that the fragrant smoke and smouldering charcoal are purifying you as you go. When you have returned to the starting point, waft some smoke over yourself and anyone else present.

CASTING THE CIRCLE

The circle is cast by drawing in etheric power through the aura and chakras, then sending it out again in a ray of directed light that you visualise as streaming forth from the tip of your athame or wand (or a pointing finger if you don't have the former).

- Begin at the north, and walk round clockwise, holding your athame or wand at arm's length in your dominant hand (the one you write with). Now begin to project a steady stream of light out through the point. As you walk slowly round the edge of the circle, "see" the light begin to form a barrier that will keep the space inside it safe. Then, when you reach the eastern point candle, start to say some words to invoke the powers of protection that will guard your magical working, as in the following:

  I call up thy power, O Circle, be thou a boundary of protection between the material world and the realm of the gods.

- Carry on till you arrive back at the north and have closed the completed circle.

CALLING IN THE QUARTERS

Calling in the quarters means calling in the elements, which are present within ourselves as well as everything else in worldly life, but which we need to focus on for our own protection and for balance within ritual and magic.

- With your wand or athame still in your hand, walk clockwise to the eastern quarter and, facing the eastern point candle, visualise the qualities of air.

- Imagine yellow light hanging in the air or burning like a light in this part of the circle, or draw a pentagram of glowing yellow light in the air before you with wand or athame. Start top left, go diagonally to bottom left, diagonally to centre right, straight across to centre left, diagonally to bottom right, diagonally to top right to join the top point, then back to bottom left. Call up the powers of air by saying something like:

  Powers of the east, powers of air, I call you into the circle to empower our rite and guard our sacred space. Hail and welcome.

- Repeat the process in each successive quarter, seeing red for south/fire, blue or blue-green for west/water, and green or brown for north/earth. Remember to imagine the qualities of each element as you reach its section of the circle.

This completes casting the circle, and you and anyone else with you are sealed into sacred space, the place between the world of everyday concerns and that of the higher realms . . . though in reality all realms coexist and interpenetrate.

RAISING ENERGY

For most magical work you will need to use some method such as singing, dancing, or drumming to raise the extra etheric energy used in magic, because you will quickly drain yourself if you try to use your own.

INVOKING THE GODDESS AND GOD

You have now come to the part of the rite when the deities are invoked, though some rituals invite them at a different point. Ask the deities you wish to work with to be present and to lend their power and protection to your work. Or use the relevant invocations if you are working with the deities mentioned in the various chapters in this book.

THE FOCUS OF THE RITE

This is the part of the ritual where the main work is done, whether that is healing, magic, or communion with the deities or other energies in the circle. This is also the point where the raised energy is used by shaping it into a pillar, sphere, stream, or cone of power that is directed toward a magical or devotional goal. Because etheric energy can be shaped so easily through creative thought, it can be imprinted with your intentions and then sent on its way to do the work you intend. If you believe in them implicitly, and if you put enough determination into them, then most magical goals will be effective. The power used can be visualised as a stream of sparking, bright, white light, or it can be given any colour you wish when using specific hues for spells.

Etheric energy is shaped by a group of people visualising themselves raising it or spinning it clockwise faster and faster till one or more participants feel it should be released. Sent forth in this way, it will eventually take root on the astral level, growing into a form that will ultimately manifest on the material plane as the result of your magical wishes. For this to be really effective, and for the spell to come about in the way you want, it's essential that you put a lot of thought and imagination into the working, being as clear and definite as you can . . . though leave a loophole by saying that you want these results if they are right for you and the best thing for all concerned, then your magic can adapt to your real needs and won't rebound on you. One or two people working without a larger group can simply direct energy with the mind, the wand, the athame, or the hands.

FEASTING

Although this is sometimes called "cakes and wine," this term stems from traditional Wiccan groups in the 1950s. Even strict Gardnerian covens now sometimes use juice in the chalice, and store-bought biscuits. Have whatever you want, from spring water and a light snack to a full-blown meal, as long as the actual blessing is done using some sort of bread, cake, or biscuit/cookie. The main purpose of eating and drinking after ritual is to give thanks to the deities and to close down the chakras, earthing any extra etheric power in the aura so that it doesn't make you feel odd, off balance, or vague later on.

- Hold up the chalice and ask for a blessing on its contents. Say something like:

  Bless this chalice, Lady, that its contents may refresh and replenish me.

  You should now drink. Then, if you are in a group, pass the chalice clockwise to the person next to you with the greeting "Blessed be."

- Any food should be placed on the pentacle and held up with a blessing such as:

  Bless this food, Lord, that it may nourish and sustain me, grounding me into the world.

  You should now take a portion of food and eat, passing the platter to the next person, saying "Blessed be."

ENDING THE RITE

Give thanks to Goddess and God for their presence and bid them farewell.

Go to the eastern quarter and see the yellow light fading, or draw a banishing pentagram, which is the opposite direction of an invoking pentagram: bottom left to top left, top right to bottom right, diagonally to left side, straight across to right side, diagonally to bottom right, and back up to the top. See the yellow pentagram being taken up till it is gone. Imagine the qualities of air fading back till they return to a normal, everyday state. Say:

Powers of the east, powers of air, thank you for attending. Hail and farewell.

Then move clockwise around the circle, doing the same with the other three elements.

This basic pattern for circle casting and ritual can be used for any rites and can be utilised and adapted to fit in with the moon phase rituals mentioned earlier in this book. Don't be afraid to experiment and change some of the order or details to suit your own way of working. The Craft is a living, evolving system with many different branches and methods, and its strength lies in variety and experimentation, so that each person can develop individualistically.

appendix b: color correspondences

The following colour correspondences can be used in candle or cord magic. The list is not exhaustive by any means, but it is a sound basis that can be built on over time with research, experimentation, and experience. Not all sources agree over correspondences, so you really have to try things out and decide for yourself what does and doesn't work for you personally.

Red: courage; passion; strength; determination; victory and success.

Orange: confidence; success; ambition; career matters; satisfying material needs; sexuality.

Yellow: communication; intellectual or mental work; study; exams; short-distance travel; good relations with neighbours or brothers and sisters.

Green: prosperity; growth; fertility; healing the natural world.

Blue: meditation; peace; tranquillity; harmony; balance; detachment; spiritual work.

Purple: wisdom; religion; philosophy; learning; higher education; long-distance travel; writing and publishing.

Pink/Mauve/Lilac/Lavender: friendship; love; passion; well-being; harmony; luxury; enjoyment; social life.

Brown: stability; earth healing; dependability.

Gold: quick money; luxury; wealth; enjoyment of the good things in life.

Silver: developing clairvoyance; purification; protection; lunar work.

White: purification; protection; peace; upliftment; can be used in place of other colours.

Black: banishing; eliminating; grounding; weight loss; dark moon meditations.

appendix c: magical tools

It is possible to get by with a minimum of equipment for rituals and magical work, and strangely enough the most essential tools are probably candles and holders to put them in. It isn't obligatory to have an athame or wand at all, as you can cast a circle mentally. However, using special equipment adds to the sense of mystery and symbolism so important to the Craft, and helps the imagination to take flight and improve magical work. Here, then, is a list of the most commonly used magical tools.

THE ATHAME

A short knife, usually with a double-sided blade and black handle. A kitchen knife is okay to use, but do keep all athames blunt to avoid accidents, and be cautious of secondhand knives that might have an unpleasant history incompatible with the love and lack of violence that is the heart of witchcraft. It is used for directing energy, as in casting the circle.

THE WAND

A piece of thin branch about the length of the forearm or longer. It can be used instead of the athame, and additionally to direct power into a spell. The woods from different trees can be fashioned into wands for various types of magic. For example: oak for strength and courage; apple for love; rowan for protection.

THE CHALICE

A cup or goblet to contain fluid for communion at the end of a rite.

THE CAULDRON

If the traditional type made from cast iron, it is a very useful, fireproof receptacle in which to place celebration or spell candles.

THE PENTACLE

A round disk about the size of a small plate. It can be made of pottery, metal, or wood, and has a pentagram inscribed on its face. The pentacle is used for placing articles ready to be blessed or consecrated, as in spell materials, or for food at the end of a rite.

THE ALTAR

A table or box on which magical tools, flowers, candles, and statues of the deities are placed during rituals. It can be a coffee table or chest that is "borrowed" for the duration of a rite, or a surface kept specially for magical work.

WATER AND SALT CONTAINERS

You need a bowl for water and something in which to keep salt ready for cleansing the circle prior to ritual. It is worth it to obtain a beautiful, special bowl and salt container to use only for this purpose.

CANDLES AND HOLDERS

Candles of different colours are used for spells and for the quarters, as well as to represent the Goddess and God on the altar. It's a good idea to have special holders for them so you don't seal yourself into the circle and work your candle spell only to find there is nothing on which to put the lighted candle afterward.

You might want to have various other things, such as a candle snuffer, cords for magic, a vase kept especially for flowers on the altar, a drum or rattle to raise energy, and statues of Goddess and God.

appendix d: moon gardening

Until the last century, gardening and other planting was very often done in accordance with the phases of the moon, and even today some people still follow this practice. In fact, at one time all tasks on a farm or in the countryside were performed in accordance with the lunar cycle, from sowing and harvesting and routine maintenance tasks to castrating or breeding livestock. This is hardly surprising in view of the effect the moon has on growth and fertility, and it is a sign of how out of touch we have become with the natural world that we now largely ignore the wisdom of our forbears, preferring to rely instead on harmful chemicals to foster productivity.

At its simplest level, moon phase gardening works on the principle that plants that bear their fruit or seed crop above ground should be planted while the moon is waxing, and those that bear root crops need to be planted on the waning moon. It is said that anything planted during the waxing moon, and especially the first week, will thrive, whereas plants put in while the moon is waning will be weak and sickly or may not survive at all. Certainly I have found this to be true myself, though I'm not much of a gardener, and I've had a rowan tree that never really thrived when it was planted the last week of the old moon, even though it was a strong, vigorous tree when I brought it home from the garden centre. However, the system can be far more complicated and comprehensive than that, with the moon's quarters being utilised, and a further subdivision being made into the astrological signs. Water signs are thought to be best for planting, though earth signs are also productive. Fire signs are used for weeding, digging, and routine tasks, while air signs are good for the thought that goes into planning out a new garden or deciding when to sow and reap or which plants to use.

NEW MOON TO FIRST QUARTER

This is the best time to sow and tend plants that bear their produce externally, such as flowers, grassy areas such as lawns, herbs, leafy salad crops, cabbages, sprouts, or corn on the cob. Now is also best for pruning and cutting, as plants are stronger and more vigorous while the moon is waxing and will therefore recover from being cut.

FIRST QUARTER TO FULL MOON

At this time plant cane fruits such as raspberries, gooseberries, red and black currants, and loganberries. This is also the best time for watery or fleshy fruits and vegetables, like melons, tomatoes, and grapes. Also sow runner and broad beans and peas now, and flowering sweet pea.

FULL MOON TO LAST QUARTER

Now is the time for root crops including carrots, turnips, parsnips, onions, radishes, beetroot, and potatoes. Spring bulbs do best planted in the waning half of the moon's cycle too, as do flowers with large fleshy roots such as irises and peonies.

LAST QUARTER TO NEW MOON

Use this period of the moon's cycle for weeding, turning the flower beds over, pruning out deadwood, and burning off garden rubbish such as leaves. Please be very careful when setting fire to an existing heap, or when forking out barrow loads to take to the fire, as creatures such as hedgehogs often nest or hibernate in piles of garden refuse.

appendix e: ogham alphabet

Letter	Ogham Name	Tree Name
B	T	beth/birch
L	⊤⊤	luis/rowan
N	⊤⊤⊤⊤	nuin/ash
F	⊤⊤⊤	fearn/alder
S	⊤⊤⊤⊤	salle/willow
H	⊥	huath/hawthorn
D	⊥⊥	duir/oak
T	⊥⊥⊥	tinne/holly
C	⊥⊥⊥⊥	coll/hazel
M	⟋	muin/vine
G	⫻	gort/ivy
Ng	⫻	ngetal/reed
R	⫻	ruis/elder

The following are included in the ogham alphabet by some authorities. They may be a later addition. Although I have not used them in my own work, they will be of interest to some readers, and I list them for the sake of completeness.

Letter	Ogham Name	Tree Name
I	ⵢ	iodho/yew
Q	ⵢ	quert/apple
E	ⵢ	eadha/aspen
Z	ⵢ	straif/blackthorn
U	ⵢ	ur/heather
O	ⵢ	onn/gorse
A	ⵢ	ailm/fir

glossary

Alexandrian
Contemporary branch of initiatory Wicca founded by Alex Sanders.

Amerterasu
Shinto sun goddess.

Anningan
Inuit moon god.

Anu
Celtic goddess of fire, fertility, and agriculture.

Anubis
Jackal-headed god of Ancient Egypt who was involved with embalming corpses and weighing the hearts of the dead in the scales of Maat.

Aphrodite
Greek goddess of love who rose from the sea. She had many amorous adventures, being irresistible to men, and this was sometimes the cause of conflict and war.

Aradia
Said to be a goddess of Etruscan legend, the daughter of Diana who came to earth to champion the poor and oppressed. She has many of the qualities of Artemis/Diana, but shows a more human face. She is much loved by British Wiccans.

Ares

Greek god of war.

Artemis

The Greek maiden goddess of the hunt, but also of midwifery. She was a lunar goddess and a goddess of the wild, of nature. Her brother was the sun god Helios/Apollo.

Astarte

Phoenician goddess based on Inanna.

Astral Plane

Plane of existence interpenetrating but less dense than the material world. Magical work is thought to take root in the astral prior to becoming manifest in the world of form.

Astrology

The analysis of a person, creature, country, or anything else by plotting the planetary patterns personal to them, and using the resulting "chart" to understand probable traits, character, and so on.

Athame

The ritual knife used to direct energy and cast the circle. Usually steel, double bladed, and with a black handle, but could be made of any other metal or stone, and with any colour for the handle. It is never used to draw blood, and the only thing that should ever be cut with it is the cake at a handfasting.

Athena

Greek goddess of wisdom and war. She was born from the head of her father, Zeus.

Aura

Sheath of subtle energy surrounding the body.

Autumn Equinox

One of the eight seasonal festivals. Second harvest. Equal days and nights but with the nights about to increase in length. Occurs around September 21.

Balder

Norse male solar deity.

Beltane

One of the eight seasonal festivals. Centres on the marriage of the Flower Maiden and the Horned Lord of the Greenwood. April 30/May 1.

Besom

Another name for the old-fashioned type of broom. It is made with twigs attached to a rough branch handle, which witches use to cleanse the perimeter of the sacred circle before ritual.

Bodhran

A round, flat, Irish hand drum, played with a double-headed wooden beater. Originally a war drum played to rouse the battle lust of Celtic warriors, the bodhran has a wild, exciting sound that can be used to quickly raise energy for magical work or ritual.

Book of Shadows

A journal of spells, rituals, dreams, meditations, and so forth kept by individual witches. It can be an actual book, a computer file, or an audiotape, for example.

Brighid (also Brigit, Brigid, Bride, Brede)

Irish solar/triple goddess of poetry, healing, and smithcraft, whose special time is the purification festival of Imbolc at the beginning of February. She was Christianised as Saint Brigit.

Buddhism

An Eastern spiritual system based on meditation and the aim of either transcending earthly existence (Tibetan and Theravada systems) or becoming spiritually enlightened whilst still in the world (Zen). It is a nontheistic system (in other words, it doesn't subscribe to the belief in deity), but teaches compassion and tolerance.

Celtic

The Bronze Age pre-Saxon people of Europe and the British Isles. They were warriors, seers, and metal workers. The four pagan fire festivals originated with them, as did the Druid priesthood, and they are well known now for their knotwork decorations. Many inhabitants of Scotland, Ireland, Wales, Cornwall, the Isle of Man, and Brittany (in northern France) are the direct descendants of the Celts, and many other Europeans and people of European ancestry have Celtic blood—which can bestow strong psychic skills.

Cerridwen

Crone goddess. She was part of Welsh legend. She owns a cauldron of transformation, and has associations with the Underworld.

Chakras

Energy centres in the auric field. Chakra is Hindu for "wheel," and these centres are said to revolve like wheels of force when activated.

Chalice

A goblet or cup used to contain wine, juice, spring water, and so forth at the end of a ritual. It belongs to the element of water.

Chandra

The Hindu moon god.

Child of Promise

The reborn sun god at Yule. Personified by such deities as the Celtic Mabon, the Persian Mithras, and Jesus.

Cone of Power

Spiral of active power shaped by witches during magical working. It can also be sphere or pillar shaped.

Corn Bride

A small figure made of wheat or other grain stalks, dressed in white to represent the reviving fertility of the crops at Imbolc.

Corn Mother

Traditionally made from the last sheaf of grain to be harvested. A small figure representing the Goddess as the Mother of the Harvest, who will retreat into the burial mounds till spring comes and the forces of growth stir again.

Coven

A small group of witches who regularly come together to work ritual and/or magic and celebrate the festivals. A close-knit coven can become something of a support group for the members, with strong bonds of love, kinship, and family growing between them.

Craft, the

Witchcraft; sometimes called the Craft of the Wise.

Crone

The aging, wise woman aspect of the Goddess. Corresponds to the waning moon.

Damuzi

A shepherd who became the lover of the goddess Inanna. He represents the crop cycle and is therefore a vegetation deity.

Demeter

Greek goddess of the corn and harvest, whose daughter Persephone was abducted by Hades and taken to the Underworld. Demeter's grieving for her daughter caused winter to come. It was only by making a pact with Hades to allow Persephone to be restored to the upper world for part of the year that Demeter felt able to let fertility and warmth come back into the world.

Diana

The Roman counterpart of the Greek goddess Artemis, Lady of the Wild.

Deity

The concept of a divine presence. Can be used to refer to a specific goddess or god form.

Divination

Obtaining insight into a situation or circumstances with the help of one of the intuitive or clairvoyant methods, such as tarot or scrying, in order to read current patterns and probable future trends.

Druid
Someone who follows the Celtic solar path of spirituality. There were Druids in ancient Europe, and modern Druidic practices are based on the possible traces of their religion; these practices were revived in the eighteenth century.

Eclipse
The blocking of the sun or moon by another heavenly body, the moon in solar eclipses, and the earth in lunar eclipses.

Elements
Part of all magical and spiritual systems. They consist of earth, air, fire, water, and ether, and are a way of experiencing and categorising the way the world we live in interfaces with the sacred.

Endymion
Selene's sleeping lover, a shepherd, whom she visits nightly in his cave.

Enlil
Sumerian Sky Father.

Ephemeris
Astronomical tables of planetary movements; an ephemeris is used for the accurate calculation of astrological charts.

Ereshkigal
Inanna's sister (who is also her darker self); ruler of the Underworld in Sumerian myth.

Etheric Energy
The psychic energy used to shape the ritual circle.

Evoke
To call forth qualities, such as aspects of deity, from oneself or another person or people during ritual.

Freya
Norse fertility goddess. She is a mother goddess, triple goddess, and the Lady of Flowers.

Gardnerian

Contemporary branch of initiatory Wicca founded by Gerald Gardner.

GMT

Abbreviation of Greenwich Mean Time, the time system based on the Greenwich Observatory, and from which all the world's time zones derive. Astrological calculations have to be converted to GMT or Universal time (which varies from GMT by a few seconds) before a horoscope can be accurately done.

Great Mother

The term used to describe the Goddess in ancient times. The Goddess as the land or the world.

Green Man

A foliate face or figure; the male spirit of growth and fertility in nature; a manifestation of the God.

Hades

The name for both the Underworld of Ancient Greek myth and its ruler.

Hag

The Goddess as ancient, wise woman. Symbolised by the dark phase of the moon just before astronomical newness. The Hag can also be a destroyer goddess such as Cerridwen, the Celtic Cailleagh, or Hecate, whose work it is to clear the way for new growth.

Hecate

Crone or Hag goddess, though she originated as a Greek lunar goddess, the keeper of the family hearth fire. She came to have two roles: by day she was a goddess of farming and fertility, but by night she became the goddess of witches and spirits, the Guardian of the Crossroads—symbolising the helper who aids in making choices when we come to a turning point in life, or when we need to let something go in order to move on.

Hephaestus

Lame Greek smith god and husband to Aphrodite, for whom he made a magical girdle.

Hindu

Religion of India. Although it has a pantheon of many different deities, it teaches that these are all aspects of the One (supreme god).

Holly King

Ancient winter aspect of the God.

Horned One

The Horned God of ancient northern Europe. Usually seen with antlers on his head, he was called Herne, Cernunnos, and Cerne. Can also refer to the Greek god Pan.

Imbolc

The festival of purification. One of the eight seasonal festivals. February 1.

Inanna

She was the Sumerian forerunner of the Egyptian Isis. She descended to the Underworld, giving up her garments and jewellery a bit at a time, symbolising her relinquishment of all outer protection, body armour, and ego masks in the search of the self. Like Isis, she is also the Queen of the Heavens and Queen of Nature, and is said to wear a rainbow as her necklace and to be crowned with stars, with the crescent moon on her brow. She has her origins in the Great Mother of ancient times, who encompassed earth, heaven, and the Underworld within her body.

Initiation

A rite of passage from one state of being to another. It can be a religious or spiritual act, such as baptism, or induction into a coven, group, or tradition; a tribal or cultural rite, such as coming into wo/manhood, graduation, marriage, and so on; or a natural phase or event, such as puberty, first sexual experience, or the death of someone close. Initiation permanently alters the consciousness of the participant, opening new doors of experience.

Invoke

To call a force or deity into oneself, another person, or ritual space by means of spoken words, or "invocations."

Isis

Egyptian goddess who stems from Inanna/Ishtar and on whom the Virgin Mary's symbolism is based. She is another manifestation of the Great Mother, a goddess of nature and the grain, whose lover, Osiris, is a dying and resurrecting vegetation god. She is Queen of the Heavens and Queen of Nature—roles that find a counterpart in the Priestess and Empress cards in tarot.

Kali

Hindu goddess of death and destruction.

Karma

Law of cause and effect. Whatever you do, for good or bad, is ultimately your responsibility, and the energy triggered by the act will come back to you eventually. This has to do with universal harmony and balance and has nothing to do with punishment (though it can feel like it sometimes).

Khensu

Ancient Egyptian lunar god.

Kwan Yin

Buddhist female Bodhisattva or saviouress, based on an ancient aspect of the Great Mother. She is a bringer of love, mercy, and compassion.

Lady, the

The Lady is the general term used to refer to the Goddess, particularly within traditional coven Wicca. It is *the* Goddess rather than any individual deity, but can also mean the Goddess as a force of nature.

Lakshmi

Hindu goddess of prosperity and fertility.

Lammas

One of the eight seasonal festivals. The first harvest. Grain harvest. Sacrifice of the God and John Barleycorn. August 1.

Lord, the

Usually meaning the Horned God of Europe, but can mean the God as a single force rather than any individual manifestation of him.

Lord of the Greenwood
The ancient Horned God or Stag King of Europe.

Lugh
Celtic god of light, originating in Ireland.

Lughnasadh
The time of Lugh, when the first harvest was cut (Lammas). In Celtic times, this was also the season for marriages and contracts.

Maat
Ancient Egyptian goddess in whose scales the hearts of the dead were weighed to determine whether or not they could go into the Afterlife.

Mabon
The Celtic name for the Autumn Equinox, named after the Mabon, the Child of Promise, who was stolen away when a baby and taken to the Underworld, but later found and returned to his birthright.

Maiden
Youthful phase of the Goddess, symbolised by the new moon.

Maiden of Flowers
Spring and early summer aspect of the Goddess.

Malina
Inuit sun goddess.

Mantra
A sacred sound or chant that is used to focus spiritual intent, especially during meditation.

Mars
Roman version of Ares, god of war.

Mercury
The Roman messenger god. His Greek counterpart was Hermes. Also the astrological planet of thought and communication.

Minerva

Roman equivalent of the Greek goddess of wisdom.

Moon's Nodes, the

Mathematical points involved with eclipses. Also used in astrology to indicate karmic emphasis in the horoscope. The north node is called Rahu and the south is called Ketu.

Mother

Fruitful phase of the Goddess, symbolised by the full moon.

Nakshatra

Lunar mansion or stage used in Indian astrology. There are twenty-seven Nakshatras, each with a different name and characteristics, and they are part of Vedic lunar astrology.

Nanna

Sumerian moon god.

Ninlil

Sumerian Earth Mother.

Norse

Meaning coming from Norway originally. Now often used to denote some of the northern traditions that follow gods and goddesses of the Nordic pantheon, such as Freya, Odin, and Loki.

Oak King

Ancient summer aspect of the God.

Oestara / Spring Equinox

One of the eight seasonal festivals. The time of rebirth in early spring. Equal day and night with the days about to increase in length. March 21.

Oracle

In ancient times, the psychic seer who spoke out at a site dedicated to prophecy. Nowadays, it can mean a form of divination such as tarot cards or runes.

Osiris
Ancient Egyptian vegetation god, Lord of the Underworld, husband to Isis.

Pentacle
A disk bearing a pentagram and, possibly, other symbols. Food, materials for spells, and so on can be placed on it on the altar. It belongs to earth.

Pentagram
Five-pointed star. It has been adopted as the symbol for witchcraft and paganism. The points represent the four elements and spirit.

Persephone
Daughter of Demeter, she was abducted by Hades and forced to stay with him in the Underworld for half the year.

Pomegranate
A round fruit in a bitter outer skin, with woody seeds inside encased in sweet pink flesh. Particularly in Greek mythology, pomegranate seeds symbolise the mystical or the divine, and may represent a knowledge that changes those who taste them. Persephone was tricked into staying with Hades in the Underworld by eating pomegranate seeds.

Prana
The life force that is present all around us, and on which we can concentrate for magical work, or increase in our own systems by breathing exercises, meditation, yoga, exercise, correct diet, and so on.

Qaballah / Kabala
Hebrew system of categorising the levels of being, spirituality, and so on. Sometimes called the Tree of Life.

Runes
A Norse and Anglo-Saxon script that is used for divination. The letters of the runic alphabet are inscribed on stones and cast in a reading, the juxtaposition and pattern of the individual letters having specific meanings.

Sacred Marriage

The Greenwood Marriage or mating of Goddess and God at Beltane. It is also the name for the union of male and female energies within Wicca, where it is undertaken between priest and priestess either as an act of sexual intercourse (usually in private, between lovers) or by lowering the athame into the chalice to bless the contents at the end of a rite or at one of the eight festivals.

Samhain

Halloween. The Feast of the Dead. The Celtic New Year. The time when the veil between the worlds is thin and we can commune with the Ancestors. October 31/November 1.

Scrying

A method of divination that uses a reflective surface such as a mirror, a bowl of water or crystal ball, smoke, and so on to defocus the mind to assist clairvoyance.

Selene

Greek moon goddess.

Shaman

A spiritual practitioner who visits other levels of being while in a trance state that has been induced by means of drumming or hallucinogens.

Skyclad

A Wiccan term meaning unclothed (wearing only the sky). Many (but by no means all) witches work ritual this way.

Smudging

Wafting incense or herbal smoke over people, objects, or ritual space to cleanse them. Much used by practitioners of the Native American paths.

Solar

Of the sun.

Solitary

A witch who works alone, by choice or because of the difficulty of finding a coven.

Soma
Indian moon god. Also the name for an elixir of life.

Summer Solstice
One of the eight seasonal festivals. Midsummer festival of the sun's maximum power. Occurs around June 21.

Tarot
A system of divination of unknown origin, comprising seventy-eight cards that represent the many aspects of life.

Themis
Greek goddess of justice; sometimes shown blindfolded and with a sword.

Thoth
Ancient Egyptian god. Originally a lunar deity, but later a god of languages, writing, and so on who helped to judge the souls of the dead.

Tree of Life
A spiritual system where occult understanding is classified according to various mutually dependant stages or stations. It has its origins in ancient times, but has become intellectualised and is now one of the foundations of the Western magical system.

Tsuki-Yoma
Shinto moon god.

Venus
The Roman interpretation of Aphrodite, though Venus is gentler and has her origins in an early agricultural goddess.

Vulcan
Roman version of Hephaestus, the lame smith god.

Wand
A short stave of wood used to direct energy in spell crafting. It can be used instead of the athame to cast the circle. It is ruled by fire.

Wheel of the Year
The round of eight festivals and the seasonal cycle.

Wiccan
Initiatory witchcraft, including Gardnerian and Alexandrian Wicca.

Yule / Winter Solstice
The sun's rebirth. One of the eight seasonal festivals. Occurs around December 21.

Yin-Yang
Chinese symbol for the balance between opposites that brings life into static harmony.

Zodiac
The band of constellations that fall within the apparent path of the sun through the skies over the course of a year. Sun sign astrology is based on these.

bibliography

Aswynn, Freya. *The Leaves of Yggdrasil*. St. Paul, Minn.: Llewellyn Publications, 1988.

Back, Philippa. *The Illustrated Herbal*. London: Hamlyn, 1987.

Baring, Anne, and Jules Cashford. *The Myth of the Goddess: Evolution of an Image*. London: Arkan/Penguin, 1993.

Beckman, Howard. *Mantras, Yantras and Fabulous Gems*. Great Britain: Balaji Publishing Co., 1997.

Campanelli, Pauline, and Dan Campanelli. *The Wheel of the Year: Living the Magical Life*. St. Paul, Minn.: Llewellyn Publications, 1990.

Campbell, Joseph. *Oriental Mythology*. New York: Penguin, 1962.

————. *The Power of Myth*. New York: Doubleday, 1988.

Carr-Gomm, Philip. *The Druid Tradition*. Shaftsbury: Element Books, 1991.

Cotterell, Arthur, and Rachell Storm. *The Ultimate Encyclopedia of Mythology*. London: Lorenz Books, 1999.

Crowley, Vivianne. *Principles of Paganism*. London: Thorsons, 1996.

————. *Wicca: The Old Religion in the New Age*. Wellingborough: The Aquarian Press, 1989.

Cunningham, Scott. *Cunningham's Encyclopedia of Magical Herbs*. St. Paul, Minn.: Llewellyn Publications, 1985.

Defouw, Hart, and Robert Svoboda. *Light on Life: An Introduction to the Astrology of India*. New Delhi: Penguin Books, 1996.

Frawley, David. *Astrology of the Seers: A Guide to Vedic/Hindu Astrology*. Twin Lakes: Lotus Press, 2000.

Gantz, Jeffrey. *The Mabinogion*. London: Penguin Books, 1976.

Graves, Robert. *The Greek Myths*. Vol. 1 and Vol. 2. London: Penguin Books, 1955.

————. *The White Goddess.* Faber & Faber Limited, 1961.

Gryffyn, Sally. *Sacred Journeys.* London: Kyle Cathie Limited, 2000.

Hand, Robert. *Planets in Transit: Life Cycles for Living.* Rockport: Para Research, 1976.

Hawke, Elen. *In The Circle: Crafting the Witches' Path.* St. Paul, Minn.: Llewellyn Publications, 2000.

————. *The Sacred Round: A Witch's Guide to Magical Practice.* St. Paul, Minn.: Llewellyn Publications, 2002.

Jordan, Michael. *Witches: An Encyclopedia of Paganism and Magic.* London: Kyle Cathie Limited, 1996.

Kindred, Glennie. *The Sacred Tree.* Stonesfield: Glennie Kindred/Counter Culture 1995.

————. *The Tree Ogham.* Stonesfield: Glennie Kindred/Counter Culture, 1997.

Levacy, William R. *Beneath a Vedic Sky: A Beginner's Guide to the Astrology of India.* Carlsbad: Astro Room, 1999.

Matthews, John, and Caitlin Matthews. *British and Irish Mythology: An Encyclopedia of Myth and Legend.* London: Diamond Books, 1995.

Murray, Liz, and Colin Murray. *The Celtic Tree Oracle: A System of Divination.* London: Rider, 1998.

Nichols, Ross. *The Book of Druidry.* London: Aquarian/Thorsons, 1990.

O'Reagan, Vivienne. *The Pillar of Isis.* London: Aquarian/Thorsons, 1992.

Stewart, R. J. *Celtic Gods Celtic Goddesses.* London: Blandford Press, 1990.

Thorsson, Edred. *The Book of Ogham: The Celtic Tree Oracle.* St. Paul, Minn.: Llewellyn Publications, 1992.

Trobe, Kala. *Invoke the Goddess: Visualisations of Hindu, Greek & Egyptian Deities.* St. Paul, Minn.: Llewellyn Publications, 2000.

Websites

http://itss.raytheon.com/cafe/qadir/amoone.html

http://members.aol.com/netgarden2/moon.html

http://news.bbc.co.uk/hi/english/sci/tech/specials/eclipse99/newsid_355000/355058.stm

http://realmagick.com/topics/87/87.html

http://www.astro.umd.edu/education/astro/moon/eclipses.html

http://www.civilization.ca/civil/egypt/egypte.html#menu

http://www.crystalinks.com/greekgods.html

http://www.earthview.com

http://www.eclipse.org.uk/lunar.htm

http://www.eclipsezone.com/tvsched.htm

http://www.enchantedencounters.com/herblist.htm

http://www.enchantedlearning.com/subjects/astronomy/sun/
solareclipses.shtml

http://www.gardeningbythemoon.com/

http://www.gpc.peachnet.edu/~pgore/astronomy/astr101/eclipses.htm

http://www.imbas.org/brighid.htm

http://www.loggia.com/myth/

http://www.mysteriousbritain.co.uk/gods&goddesses/celtic.html

http://www.paganspath.com/magik/moon.htm#gardening

http://www.pendevil.com/greekgods.asp

http://www.stariq.com/pagetemplate/article.asp?pageid=861

http://www.thursdaysclassroom.com/index_12aug99.html

http://www.touregypt.net/godsofegypt/thoth.htm

http://www.usfca.edu/westciv/Sumerian.html

http://www.witchs-brew.com/shadows/goddess/

http://www.exploratorium.edu/eclipse/

index

Hag, 2, 27, 114, 135, 157

harvest, 13–14, 17, 41, 48, 58, 120, 133, 152, 154–155, 159–160

Hasta, 92–93

Hathor, 55

hawthorn, 126, 130, 149

hazel, 132–133, 149

heather, 150

Hecate, 2–3, 5, 104, 106–107, 110, 114, 157

Helios, 48, 152

Hellenic, 80, 112

Hephaestus, 35, 37, 157, 164

herbs, 42, 52, 70, 137, 148

Hermes, 43, 112, 160

Hermit, the, 29

Herne, 60, 158

holly, 22, 131–132, 149, 158

Holly King, 131, 158

Horned God, 60, 88, 106, 158–160

Horus, 55–57

Huath, 130, 149

hunter goddess, 2, 45

Imbolc, 6, 127, 153–154, 158

Inanna, 6, 12–16, 35, 37, 48, 51–52, 55, 60, 106, 111, 152, 155–156, 158–159

India, 4, 26, 59, 83, 101, 110, 158, 166–167

Indian, 4, 32, 42, 60, 83–102, 106, 110, 161, 164

Indra, 94–95

initiation, 13, 21, 67–76, 122, 127, 158

invoke, 15, 17, 62, 79, 140, 158

Irish, 6, 153

Ishtar, 12, 16, 55, 159

Isis, 3, 6, 10–12, 16, 35, 38, 48, 55–58, 60, 62, 78, 158–159, 162

Islamic, 41

Italy, 49

Japan, 2, 38, 41

Jesus, 12, 50, 154

Jupiter, 31, 89, 94, 99, 122, 124

Justice, 78, 80, 121, 164

Jyeshta, 95–96

Ka'abah stone, 41

Kali, 106, 110, 114, 159

karma, 32, 159

Ketu, 26, 31–32, 84–85, 91, 96, 161

Khensu, 43, 159

King of the Forest, 131

Krittika, 87

Kundalini, 100

Kwan Yin, 34, 37–38, 159

kyphi, 122

Lady, the, 159

Lakshmi, 48, 59–60, 159

Lammas, 132, 159–160

Last Quarter, 77–82, 113, 148

Legend of the Descent of the Goddess, 13

Leo, 90–92, 120

ley energy, 133

Libra, 93–94, 121

Lord, the, 159

lotus, 37, 59, 62, 95, 166

Lucifer, 50

Luis, 125, 127, 136, 149

lunar, 2–4, 6–9, 12, 23–27, 31–34, 41–45, 48, 50–51, 55, 57, 59, 61, 64–65, 77, 79, 83–103, 111, 125, 129, 133, 136, 144, 147, 152, 156–157, 159, 161, 164

Indian lunar zodiac, 83–102

Maat, 43, 78–80, 112, 151, 160

Mabon, 133, 154, 160

Madalena, 49–50

Magha, 91

magical journal, 8

magical name, 68

Maiden, 2, 5, 9, 16, 19, 37, 57, 107, 152–153, 160

Malina, 42, 160

Mars, 37, 88, 93, 98, 118, 122, 160

Mary, 12, 38, 55, 159

Mary Magdalene, 12

medieval, 43, 83

menstruation, 2

Mercury, 43, 90, 95, 101, 119, 121, 160

Metta, 38

Midsummer, 124, 131, 164

midwifery, 6, 10, 152

Milky Way, the, 15

Minerva, 6, 161

Mitra, 95

moon gardening, 147

Moon God, 4, 12, 41–43, 151, 154, 161, 164

moon phase, 19, 38, 43, 137, 143, 147

moon's cycle, 6, 13, 18, 34–35, 39, 111, 113, 116, 148

moon's nodes, 26, 30–31, 84, 161

moon's shadow, 23–25

mooncakes, 19, 41, 62

Mother, 2–3, 11–12, 15, 27, 42, 48, 55, 57–58, 60, 62, 80, 106, 110, 113, 119, 154, 156–159, 161

Mother, the, 27, 55, 57, 157

Mother of Christ, 12

Mountain Ash, 127

Mrigashira, 88

Muin, 133, 149

Mula, 96

Nakshatras, 83–85, 97, 101, 161

Nanna, 12, 43–44, 161

Near East, 41, 55

Neolithic, 106

Nepthys, 55–56

Neptune, 124

New Age, 26

new moon, 5–19, 23, 34, 44, 48, 51–52, 60, 62, 79, 103, 107, 111, 113, 116, 125, 148, 160

Ngetal, 134, 149

Nile, 43, 55–56

Nile Valley, 43, 56

Ninlil, 3, 44, 161

Nirriti, 96

Nordic, 15, 41, 161

Norse, 128, 153, 156, 161–162

Nuin, 125, 128, 136

Oak, 131, 136, 145, 149, 161

Oak King, 131, 161

Oestara, 161

ogham alphabet, 126, 136, 149–150

old moon, 5, 103–116, 147

Osiris, 12, 55–56, 60, 112, 159, 162

Otherworld, 127

Oxford, 21

pagan, 26, 50, 55, 126, 153

Pan, 60, 114–115, 133, 158

Paphos, 35

Paps of Anu, 59

Path of Totality, 24

pentacle, 138–139, 143, 146, 162

pentagram, 74, 141, 143, 146, 162

penumbra, 23–24

Persephone, 6, 12, 57–58, 155, 162

Pharaoh, 78

Phoenician, 152

Pisces, 99–101, 117, 123–124